CFA® Level I
Study Guide

2014

BPP House
142-144 Uxbridge Road
London W12 8AA

Tel: 0845 0751 100 (within UK)
+44 (020) 8740 2211 (overseas)

learningmedia@bpp.com
www.bpp.com/learningmedia

Published December 2013

ISBN 9781 4727 0412 2
eISBN 978 1 4727 0436 8

British Library Cataloguing-in-Publication Data
A catalogue record for this book
is available from the British Library

Published by

BPP Learning Media Ltd
BPP House, Aldine Place
London W12 8AA

www.bpp.com/learningmedia

Printed in United Kingdom by Ricoh
Ricoh House, Ullswater Crescent
Coulsdon CR5 2HR

Your learning materials, published by BPP Learning Media Ltd, are
printed on paper obtained from traceable sustainable sources.

Dear Customer

What does the little © mean and why does it matter?
Your market-leading BPP books, course materials
and e-learning materials do not write and update
themselves. People write them: on their own behalf
or as employees of an organisation that invests in
this activity. Copyright law protects their livelihoods.
It does so by creating rights over the use of the
content.

Breach of copyright is a form of theft – as well being
a criminal offence in some jurisdictions, it is
potentially a serious beach of professional ethics.

With current technology, things might seem a bit
hazy but, basically, without the express permission
of BPP Learning Media:

- Photocopying our materials is a breach of
  copyright
- Scanning, ripcasting or conversion of our
  digital materials into different file formats,
  uploading them to facebook or emailing
  them to your friends is a breach of
  copyright

You can, of course, sell your books, in the form in
which you have brought them – once you have
finished with them. (Is this fair to your fellow
students? We update for a reason.)

And what about outside the UK? BPP Learning Media
strives to make our materials available at prices
students can afford by local printing arrangements,
pricing policies and partnerships which are clearly
listed on our website. A tiny minority ignore this and
indulge in criminal activity by illegally photocopying
our material or supporting organisations that do. If
they act illegally and unethically in one area, can you
really trust them?

BPP
LEARNING MEDIA

Using the Study Guide

Your Study Guide has been created to help you navigate your way to the most important elements of the CFA Level I Official Curriculum books. The biggest challenge when working through these books is to understand where the high priority content can be found. The study guides that follow take each Reading Assignment in the curriculum and provide

- A priority level

- Suggested study time

- Guidance regarding online resources

- An overview of key areas to focus on within the Readings

- Referenced to recommended exam focussed examples and end of chapter questions in the CFA books.

This study guide document is designed to highlight the best use of the CFA books, and should be read through before studying each reading. At a minimum, all recommended exercises and questions should be attempted.

In addition you should ensure you make the best use of the other supporting BPP materials (not included in the suggested study hours):

Essential Formulas: Use this to outline the must-learn formulae and to test your knowledge.

Passcards: Use to provide a summarised version of the curriculum, ideal for carrying around and reviewing key content of the readings.

Study Session Maps: Use as a basis for your own summaries of the study sessions to help retain key knowledge.

Question Bank: Comprehensive syllabus coverage in both hard copy and online versions. These should be attempted after working through the Readings and the CFA end of chapter questions. Time spent working through question practice is not included in the suggested study hours. As a guide total study time should be 250 – 300 hours, which builds in at least 100 hours of question practice and consolidation.

Progress Tests: 10 exam standard tests to check your understanding and application.

Half-Way There Mock Exam: A 3-hour paper designed to test your knowledge half-way through your studies.

Practice Examinations: Three full 6 hour papers designed to test your readiness for the exam and identify any areas of weakness that need some last minute revision.

Key Level I Exam Details

Exam Dates

The Level I exam is available twice a year, at the start of June and December, typically on the first Saturday (see CFAI website for confirmation).

Exam Format

The Level I exam will consist of 240 multiple choice questions, 120 in the three-hour morning session and 120 in the three-hour afternoon session. All topic areas are covered in both the morning and afternoon sessions.

Guideline Topic Area Weights

CFA Institute has provided the following guideline topic area weights for the Level I exam.

Topic Area	Guideline Weight (%)
Ethical and Professional Standards	15
Investment Tools	
Quantitative Methods	12
Economics	10
Financial Reporting and Analysis	20
Corporate Finance	8
Investment Tools Total	50
Asset Classes	
Equity Investments	10
Fixed Income	12
Derivatives	5
Alternative Investments	3
Asset Classes Total	30
Portfolio Management and Wealth Planning	5
TOTAL	100

Results will be emailed to candidates within 60 days of the exam (the exact date is published on the CFAI website a few weeks after the exam). The email is sent out after 09:00 EST and can arrive at any time during the day. The day after the emails have been sent, the results are made available online on the CFAI website.

Exam Enrolment

The simplest way to enrol for your Level I exam is to do so via the CFA Institute website www.cfainstitute.org.

The final deadline for exam enrolments is approximately three months prior to the examination (early March for the June sitting and early September for the December sitting). However, you will pay a lower enrolment fee if you enrol in advance of the final deadlines – see CFA website for exam dates and fees.

Calculator Policy

CFA Institute approves the use of only two models of calculator in the CFA examinations.

- Texas Instruments (TI) BAII Plus (including the BAII Plus Professional)
- Hewlett Packard (HP) HP12C (including the HP12C Platinum)

Additional Exam-Related Information

CFA Institute emails Candidate Newsletters containing important information related to the exam process. These Candidate Newsletters are also posted on the CFA Institute website www.cfainstitute.org. You will also find information related to your exam admission ticket, identification documents that you need to bring for the exam and information on what you are allowed to bring with you into the exam centre in the Candidate Newsletters.

CFA Institute also provide sample and mock exams for you to purchase and attempt online from their website. These sample and mock exams cover the current CFA curriculum and contain questions from the past exams.

Useful Website Links and BPP Contact Details

CFA Institute website	www.cfainstitute.org
Candidate Preparation Toolkit	www.cfainstitute.org/cfaprog/resources/
CFA Society of the UK	www.cfauk.org
BPP Learning Media	0845 0751 100 (within UK)
	44 (0) 20 8740 2211 (overseas)

Registered Trademarks

CFA® and Chartered Financial Analyst® and Global Investment Performance Standards (GIPS®) are trademarks owned by CFA Institute. CFA Institute does not endorse, promote, review or warrant the accuracy of the products or services offered by BPP.

Contents

STUDY GUIDANCE

Ethical and Professional Standards

This guidance aims to identify the topics that we consider to be of premium importance for your exam preparation.

Study session 1 (Volume 1) comprises of:

Reading 1   Code of Ethics and Standards of Professional Conduct

Reading 2   Guidance for Standards I – VII

Reading 3   Introduction to the Global Investment Performance Standards

Reading 4   Global Investment Performance Standards

Recommended study time is 13.5 hours of work. An additional 2 hours should be added to complete Progress Test 1.

 ## Exam focus

Ethical and Professional Standards are tested in both the morning and afternoon papers. There will be 18 questions in each paper representing 15% of the overall exam. These will be the first set of questions in each paper. Up to 3 questions in each paper will be on the Global Investment Performance Standards (GIPS).

The main focus of the examination will be on the CFA Institutes Professional Standards and understanding the details of the standards.

To do well in this section you have to know the Standards in order to be able to determine if in the questions somebody is complying with the standards and if not which standards they are not compliant with.

There is an 'Ethics Adjustment' applied by the CFA institute for candidates that are near the passing score, and do especially well in this section.

Ethics also forms 10% of the exam for Level II and III, so there is a high amount of knowledge transfer. Make sure you become an ethics expert for Level I and this will set you in good stead for what follows.

This section in total comprises about 250 pages in the CFA study book but it is not necessary to go into all the details in order to meet the learning outcomes required in the exam.

 ## Pre-requisites

There are no pre-requisites to this Study Session.

Candidates who work in financial services and have knowledge of local regulatory rules cannot rely on this as the CFA Standards and the focus of the examination will be very different.

Key areas

- Understand the structure of the CFAI Professional Conduct Program and the associated disciplinary process.

- Know the six components of the Code of Ethics and the seven Standards of Professional Conduct.

- Be able to summarise the ethical responsibilities of the Code and Standards.

Content review – CFA curriculum

The chapter starts with a history of the evolution of the professional standards and details the changes from the previous edition. This is not of importance.

The next section, 'CFA Institute Professional Conduct Program' is a short section but is frequently examined.

The 'Adoption of the Codes' section is not important and the section following, 'Why Ethics Matters' is largely common sense.

1 hour

The last section in the chapter lists the Code of Ethics and the Standards of Professional Conduct. Although this section is key and provides the precursor to the guidance for each Standard, it is referred to in much more detail in Reading 2.

You will not be tested on Standard numbers but knowing the headings can really help you learn the detail associated with each Standard.

Question practice

- There are no questions at the end of this reading. The learning outcome statements for this reading are tested within the questions at the back of Reading 2.

Key areas

- For Standards I-VII, understand the guidance and application of each and every Standard.

- The recommended procedures for compliance are only of moderate importance.

Content review – CFA curriculum

STANDARD I – PROFESSIONALISM (page 19)

The section is broken up into the four sub-sections of this Standard:

A. Knowledge of the Law
B. Independence and Objectivity
C. Misrepresentation
D. Misconduct

A. Knowledge of the Law (page 19)

There are three sections which should be read:

- Relationship between the Code and Standards and applicable law.

- Participation in or association with violations by others.

- Exhibit 1 Global applications of the Code and Standards is a good summary which covers all combinations of which laws apply under which circumstances.

Of less importance are the recommended procedures for compliance although it is suggested that this section is read briefly.

The Application of the Standard examples that then follow are far more detailed than the exam questions. They are however a good revision guide and it is recommended that you read through examples 1-7, trying to draw conclusions yourself before reading the comments.

8 hours

B. Independence and Objectivity (page 27)

This standard is often one in which candidates get confused as there are different rules for different relationships. It is worth spending extra time in order to understand the rules relating to these relationships as it is an area that is consistently examined in detail.

You must read and understand the statement relating to Independence and Objectivity and need to read the following sections:

- Guidance
- Buy side clients
- Fund manager relationships
- Investment banking relationships
- Public companies
- Credit rating agency opinions
- Issuer paid research
- Travel funding

Of less importance are the recommended procedures for compliance although it is suggested that this section is read briefly.

The Application of the Standard examples that then follow are again far more detailed than the exam questions. There are 12 examples which illustrate the wide variety of examinable areas under this Standard. It is recommended that you read through at least 1 example relating to each area, if not all of them, trying to draw conclusions for yourselves before reading the comments.

C. Misrepresentation (page 37)

You need to understand the three areas covered:

- Impact on investment practice
- Plagiarism
- Work completed for employer

Make sure you understand where violations have not been committed and why.

Again, the recommendations are not key but working through the applications is necessary.

You probably do not need to work through all the plagiarism examples but it is recommended you work through as many examples as possible.

D. Misconduct (page 46)

This is a short section and should be read through completely including all the applications.

STANDARD II – INTEGRITY OF CAPITAL MARKETS (page 48)

There are two sub-sections:

A.   Material non-public information
B.   Market manipulation

A. Material Non-Public Information (page 48)

You need to read through this section focusing on what is deemed material information (look at the bullet points and making sure you understand the Mosaic theory.

The application examples cover a wide range of scenarios but you do not need to work through all the examples covering acting on non-public information.

B. Market Manipulation (page 58)

This is a short section. Read the guidance section in particular and make sure you understand what is meant by market manipulation. Work through the example applications.

STANDARD III – DUTIES TO CLIENTS (page 62)

This has five sections:

A.   Loyalty, prudence and care (page 62)
B.   Fair dealing (page 70)
C.   Suitability (page 77)
D.   Performance presentation (page 83)
E.   Preservation of confidentiality (page 86)

A. Loyalty, Prudence and Care

This covers the concept that the client's interests are paramount. It is important to understand the prudence aspect and the CFA requirements as this is not always as clear as what is meant by loyalty or care.

Read through the text including the recommended procedures and work through examples 1-7. If you have time look at the last two examples as well.

B. Fair Dealing

Understand what is meant by the term 'fair' and how this applies to investment recommendations and actions. Look at examples 1, 3, 4, 6 and 7.

C. Suitability

Read carefully the definition in bold and focus on the sections about developing an investment policy and understanding the client's risk profile.

Exam Tip

The exam will often test your knowledge of this section by asking questions in which a non-suitable investment makes money for a client and asking whether the investment manager has done anything wrong. If you read this section you will see that usually they have.

It is worth reading all the examples making sure you understand the solutions.

D. Performance Presentation

You need only read through this section quickly, mainly the section, 'Compliance without applying GIPS Standards'. The concepts are covered in much more detail in Global Investment Performance Standards in Readings 3 and 4.

E. Preservation of Confidentiality

This is a short section which most find easy to understand. Only a quick read through is needed including the applications.

STANDARD IV – DUTIES TO EMPLOYERS (page 89)

There are three sections:

A.   Loyalty
B.   Additional compensation arrangements
C.   Responsibility of supervisors

A. Loyalty (page 89)

This is an area which is consistently examined in particular, independent practice and leaving an employer.

Read through the section but you do not need to read the recommended procedures.

Work through the examples.

Exam Tip

Do not always assume that the employee or individual has always done something wrong. Make sure you understand what they can do as well as what they can't. Look at examples 7, 9, 10 and 12.

B. Additional Compensation Arrangements (page 97)

This is a short section which can be gone through quickly. Make sure you understand the circumstances and procedures in which CFA members can accept additional compensation.

Work through all three examples.

C. Responsibilities of Supervisors (page 99)

Read through the section, skipping the recommended procedures. Work through examples 1 - 4.

STANDARD V – INVESTMENT ACTIONS ANALYSIS RECOMMENDATIONS AND ACTIONS (page 105)

There are three sections:

A.   Diligence and reasonable basis
B.   Communications with clients
C.   Record retention

This is one of the more straight forward Standards.

A. Diligence and reasonable Basis (page 105)

Focus on the first section covering due diligence and also understand how third party quantitative research can be used. It is only necessary to work through examples 1 - 8 to get a good all round coverage but do read through the other examples if you have time.

B. Communications with Clients and Prospective Clients (page 114)

Read through the section and make sure in particular you understand the distinction between facts and opinions. This is often examined. You need only work through examples 1 - 4. The later examples only reiterate the same principals.

C. Record Retention (page 119)

This section is short and straight forward and only needs a quick read through.

STANDARD VI – CONFLICTS OF INTEREST (page 121)

This is a short standard containing three sections:

A.   Disclosure of conflicts
B.   Priority of transactions
C.   Referral fees

A. Disclosure of Conflicts (page 121)

Understand the difference as well as the similarities between disclosure to clients and disclosure to employers.

Work through examples 1, 2, 5, 7, 8 and 11.

B. Priority of Transactions (page 128)

This is an easier section for most to understand. Read through the section, skipping the recommended actions and read quickly through the examples which you should find straight forward. Make sure that you understand the difference in example 3 from the other examples.

C. Referral Fees (page 133)

A short section which can be read through quickly. Look at the examples and make sure that you understand the solution to example 5 and why it is different to the other examples.

STANDARD VII – RESPONSIBILITIES AS A CFA INSTITUTE MEMBER OR CFA CANDIDATE (page 137)

You can be guaranteed there will be some questions on this Standard. It is a CFA exam and they want candidates to understand their responsibilities.

A. Conduct as Members and Candidates in the CFA Program (page 137)

The rules of Conduct should be obvious and you should be able to read through this section quickly. The bullet points within the guidance section provide a good summary. Note however the rules about expressing an opinion. If you feel comfortable with this section you need not go through all the examples.

B. Reference to the CFA Institute, CFA Designation, and the CFA program (page 142)

This section is not as straight forward because there are some subtle differences between what is allowed and what is not allowed. You should read the text and then Exhibits 3 and 4 which provide a very good summary of the rules and their application. Attempt to answer one or two of the example questions.

Question practice

- Questions 1 - 40 cover a wide variety of examinable areas and students should attempt all questions. It is recommended that you attempt these questions in two sessions of twenty questions each, leaving the second set of questions until later on as a revision guide. If you are having to guess at the answers consistently, revise by going through the summaries at the end of each section.

2 hours

- Students should seek to understand reasoning behind the answers where they have not got the question right or guessed at the answer.

Additional resources

Document: Bad ethical behaviour (examples of real life ethical violation as reported in CFA Institute Magazine).

Ethics presentation from CFA: document detailing how to view an online presentation from CFA Institute with descriptions of the standards and additional questions.

Key areas

The CFA has increased the emphasis on GIPS in recent exams and it is likely you will receive 3 questions out of the 18 in total in both the morning and afternoon exams on GIPS. If you understand the key areas, which are not that extensive, you will be well placed to answer all the questions and there are large amounts of details that you need not study.

- Understand the reasons for GIPS, who they apply to and what they are used for/who benefits.
- Understand the objective of the GIPS executive Committee.
- Understand the key characteristics of GIPS.
- Understand historical performance rules.
- Be able to describe the nine major sections of the GIPS Standards.

Content review – CFA curriculum

Reading 3 (page 167)

Read through this very short section to gain an overview of GIPS and understand why they were introduced and for whom. Make sure you read carefully the verification section.

Reading 4 (page 171)

You do not need to know the history of GIPS. Start with the 'Introduction' section

Read thoroughly the following sections:

- Overview
- Historical performance record
- Compliance
- Effective date
- Implementing a global Standard

2 hours

You do not need to know the country sponsors.

Read through the section on 'Provisions of GIPS' thoroughly making sure you can list the nine standards and their core characteristics.

What follows is a lot of detail on the nine GIP Standards. It is recommended that you read only section '0, Fundaments of Compliance' noting the requirements and the recommendations.

After this we consider the rest of the chapter very low priority and not necessary to go through. This detail is tested at Level III.

You may find it useful to look at the example presentation in Appendix 4A, to help put it all into perspective.

Question practice

- Attempt the three practice problems.

30 minutes

- In addition, all questions in the BPP Question Bank should be attempted prior to the exam.

CHECKPOINT – END OF STUDY SESSION 1

You are now able to attempt the **Progress Test 1 on Ethical and Professional Standards**. **2 hours**

NOTES

Progress Test 1 – Ethical and Professional Standards

Unless otherwise stated in the question, all individuals in the following questions are CFA Institute members or candidates in the CFA program and are therefore subject to CFA Institute Code of Ethics and Standards of Professional Conduct.

Subsequent references to CFA Institute Code of Ethics and Standards of Professional Conduct will read Code and Standards.

Questions

1. John Maple recently left his employer to start a new business. He did not sign a non-compete agreement with his old employer and is operating in the same industry. When he leaves, he contacts his old clients to tell them of his new business, using the telephone directory to obtain their telephone numbers. Which one of the following statements regarding Maple's conduct is *most appropriate*?

    A. Maple has breached Standard V.B Communication with Clients and Prospective Clients by contacting clients using the phone book.

    B. Maple has breached both Standard IV.A Loyalty and Standard V.B Communication with Clients and Prospective Clients.

    C. Maple has not breached any Standards.

2. Lucy Clarke is a portfolio manager for Galaxy Investment Managers. Galaxy is a large money manager, looking after funds in excess of $100 million. She undertakes a large amount of voluntary work in her spare time and has recently become a trustee of a charity that has funds of $1 million. Although the fund is relatively small, the importance of the fund to the charity means that all investment decisions are thoroughly researched, a time-consuming task but one that Clarke enjoys. Which one of the following statements regarding Clarke's conduct is *most appropriate*?

    A. Clarke has breached Standard IV.A Loyalty by undertaking work in competition with her employer.

    B. Clarke has breached Standard VI.A Disclosure of Conflicts by not informing her employer of a time-consuming role that requires her to make investment decisions.

    C. Clarke has not breached any Standards.

3. Diana Jones is an analyst working for ABC Investment Advisers. One of ABC's clients in the mergers and acquisitions department is XYZ Inc. and ABC's President is a director of XYZ. Jones has been asked to write a report on XYZ. Which one of the following courses of action is *most appropriate*?

    A. Do not write a report due to the directorship held by ABC's President.

    B. Write a report of a purely factual nature.

    C. Write a report but disclose in it the relationship between ABC and XYZ.

4. According to the Code and Standards an investment adviser should update his knowledge about a client's circumstances at least:

    A. Every six months.

    B. Annually.

    C. Every 18 months.

5. Which one of the following is *least likely* to be a breach of Standard II.B – Market Manipulation?

    A. Spreading a rumour about the poor health of a company's CEO to depress its share price.

    B. Transacting in back-to-back buy/sell strategies in order to exploit tax loopholes.

    C. Presenting the price of a security by issuing a misleading statement.

6. Scott Blair is an analyst at Ice Investment Company. He is currently working closely with Volcano Inc, a chocolate company that is in the process of preparing for a secondary equity offering. Blair is taking part in a conference call with Volcano, who are discussing the failed launch of a new product. The failed launch will result in a significant drop in earnings. Throughout the call, members of the Ice sales team are wandering in and out of Blair's office and hear the information about the failed launch and earnings fall. As a result, they sell stock from client, proprietary and employee accounts. Which of the following statements is *most appropriate*?

    A. Blair has not breached Standard II.A Material Nonpublic Information because he did not trade on the information or encourage the sales team to do so, but the sales team has breached Standard II.A Material Nonpublic Information by trading on the information.

    B. Blair has not breached Standard II.A Material Nonpublic Information because he did not trade on the information or encourage the sales team to do so, and the sales team has not breached Standard II.A Material Nonpublic Information because they did not misappropriate the information.

    C. Blair has breached Standard II.A Material Nonpublic Information because he did not prevent the transfer of the information and the sales team has breached Standard II.A Material Nonpublic Information by trading on the information.

7. Which of the following *best describes* the Mosaic Theory?

    A. An analyst combines material public information with immaterial nonpublic information to come to a material conclusion about a company. Acting on this conclusion would constitute insider trading.

    B. An analyst combines material public information with material nonpublic information to come to a material conclusion about a company. Acting on this conclusion would constitute insider trading.

    C. An analyst combines material public information with immaterial nonpublic information to come to a material conclusion about a company. Acting on this conclusion would not constitute insider trading.

8. Which of the following statements regarding Global Investment Performance Standards (GIPS) is *least accurate*?

   A. The GIPS standards are explicitly incorporated in the Code of Ethics and Standards of Professional Conduct.

   B. One of the stated objectives of the GIPS standards is to obtain worldwide acceptance of a standard for the calculation and presentation of investment performance in a fair, comparable format that provides full disclosure.

   C. Some aspects of the GIPS standards are mandatory (i.e. they must be followed to claim compliance); other aspects are recommended (i.e. they should be followed).

9. The term 'material' in the phrase 'material nonpublic information' refers to information that is likely to significantly affect the market price of the issuing company's securities, or that is:

   A. Likely to preclude the financial analyst or the analyst's firm from rendering unbiased or objective advice.

   B. Acquired by the financial analyst from a special or confidential relationship with the issuing company.

   C. Likely to be considered important by reasonable investors in determining whether to trade a particular security.

10. Which of the following is *least accurate* with respect to the scope and purpose of verification under the GIPS standards?

    A. Verification is mandatory and a firm must perform its own verification.

    B. Verification tests whether the firm has complied with all the composite construction requirements of GIPS on a firm-wide basis.

    C. The primary objective of verification is to establish that a firm claiming compliance with the GIPS standards has adhered to the standards.

11. Jane Doe is a junior research analyst with Howard & Sons, a brokerage and investment banking firm. Howard's mergers and acquisitions department, which handles mergers and acquisitions, has represented Britland Company in all its acquisitions for the past 20 years. Two of Howard's senior officers are directors of various Britland subsidiaries. Doe has been asked to write a research report on Britland. In the context of the Code and Standards, what is Doe's best course of action?

    A. Doe may write the report provided the officers agree not to alter it.

    B. Doe may write the report if she discloses Howard & Sons' special relationship with Britland in the report.

    C. Doe may write the report but must refrain from expressing any opinions because of the special relationships between the two companies.

12. Adam Long, an equity analyst, has got a one-off freelance assignment with Caspian, a fund management firm, whose CEO he knows from previous employment. The assignment is a report on Agala Inc, which was agreed over a meal and sealed with a handshake. Just before completing the task he is offered an interview for a full-time analyst position at a leading equity house. To impress them with the quality of his work, he is thinking of showing them the work he has done on Agala. Which of the following statements is *most appropriate*?

   A. Long should not disclose his work even though he has no written contract with Caspian. To do so would be a likely breach of Standard IV.A – Loyalty.

   B. Long can show his work to his prospective employer because it is his work which he has not yet shown to Caspian and he has no written contract with Caspian.

   C. Long must disclose his work to his prospective employer as not to do so would be a breach of Standard VI.A – Disclosure of Conflicts, which requires disclosure of all matters of potential interest to potential employers.

13. Paula Yavy, a senior equity analyst at Hollander, has recently completed some research into Casco Inc and concluded that the stock should go on Hollander's buy list. Following well documented internal procedures she calls a team meeting and notifies her subordinates of her decision. One of her team, knowing it is against the firm's rules, buys stocks in Casco for their own account. Yavy does not become aware of this action. Which of the following statements is *most appropriate*?

   A. Yavy has breached Standard VI.A – Responsibilities of Supervisors as she should not have allowed one of her team to trade the stock based on her buy recommendation.

   B. Yavy has not breached Standard VI.A – Responsibilities of Supervisors as she was following well documented procedures to prevent what happened from happening.

   C. Yavy has breached Standard VI.A – Responsibilities of Supervisors as she failed to supervise reasonably and adequately the actions of those she supervises.

14. Which of the following statements is *most appropriate* under Standard IV.A – Loyalty?

   A. Members are prohibited from contacting former clients once they have left the firm.

   B. Consent from the employer is necessary to permit independent practice that could conflict with the interest of the firm.

   C. Firm work stored on a home computer, with the knowledge of the firm, becomes the employee's property when they leave the firm.

15. Which one of the following is *least likely to be an* objective of the Global Investment Performance Standards (GIPS)?

   A. To bolster the notion of self-regulation.

   B. Ensure performance data is accurate and consistent on a country by country basis.

   C. Enable fair global competition among investment firms without creating barriers to entry for new firms.

16. Fred Connor is a precious metals analyst for Alpha Securities and has just finished a report on Gamma Gold mining Inc. In the report he has included an estimate of the gold reserves of Gamma's mines. Connor arrived at his estimation based on sample drilling information released by the company. In his opinion, the company has large reserves. On the back of his estimation he has made a buy recommendation. Which of the following standards is *most likely* to have been breached?

    A. Standard III.A – Loyalty, Prudence and Care.

    B. Standard IV.C – Responsibilities of Supervisors.

    C. Standard V.A – Diligence and Reasonable Basis.

17. Neil Smith is on a business trip to Japan to meet the management of one of the firms that he covers as a research analyst. He is currently rating the company as a 'buy'. While in a meeting, he is informed by the management that they are anticipating significant delivery problems at most of their factories and that this will have a negative impact on sales. No other analyst currently knows this information. Which of the following statements is *most accurate*?

    A. Smith must change his recommendation to a sell, as to not include the information would breach his fiduciary duty to his clients.

    B. Smith must not change his recommendation under any circumstances as to do so would breach the Code and Standards on the use of material nonpublic information.

    C. Smith should encourage the company to disseminate the news to the market before publishing his own updated recommendation.

18. Which one of the following is most likely to conflict with CFA Institute Code and Standards?

    A. Analysts may change their investment recommendations without obtaining approval from their supervisor.

    B. Personal account transactions by analysts should not be scrutinized for confidentiality reasons.

    C. A portfolio manager should conduct a fact-find about a new customer before undertaking investment action on the customer's behalf.

19. John Sanchez's business card refers to himself as 'CFA candidate'. Janet Connor's business card does not make reference to her participation in the CFA program. However, her resumé states that she is a Level II CFA candidate, having sat and passed Level I of the program and being registered to sit Level II at the next sitting.

    Who, if any, have breached CFA Institute Code and Standards?

    A. Connor and Sanchez.

    B. Connor only.

    C. Sanchez only.

20. Burt Hoffman is a portfolio manager who has the pension plan of a company as an account. The company's directors are asking him to vote in their favour at a forthcoming stakeholders' meeting. Since the account is a large one, Hoffman does not wish to offend the directors and risk losing it.

   In addition, Hoffman puts the transactions of the account through a broker who gives Hoffman useful investment advice on European equities. This information is of no use in relation to the pension plan account but is useful for other accounts. The broker gives best execution and offers very low commissions.

   Hoffman reviews the arguments for and against the directors and decides that the balance of argument is in their favour and votes for them. Which of the following statements is *most appropriate*?

   A. Hoffman has violated Standards by voting for the directors.

   B. Hoffman has violated Standards by using the broker for the account's transactions.

   C. Hoffman has not violated Standards.

21. If any part of Global Investment Performance Standards (GIPS) is in conflict with local laws, which of the following statements is *most accurate*?

   A. The firm must follow the local laws where relevant, but can still claim compliance with the GIPS as long as the conflict is disclosed.

   B. The firm can claim compliance with the GIPS standards, but must go against the local laws.

   C. The firm can follow the local laws and still claim compliance with the GIPS even if they have not followed any of the GIPS standards.

22. Which of the following is *most appropriate* with respect to Standard I.A – Knowledge of the Law for an analyst who is a CFA Institute member operating overseas, where the local laws are less strict than US laws and CFA Institute Code and Standards and where local laws apply?

   A. The analyst must follow local laws because they are less strict than US law and CFA Institute Code and Standards.

   B. The analyst must follow the appropriate international laws, since there is a conflict between the level of severity of local and US laws and regulations.

   C. The analyst must follow CFA Institute Code and Standards since they are stricter than the local laws.

23. Matthew Brown has just completed a quantitative analysis of stock returns relative to book value for a number of stocks over the last year. Ben Evans has just overheard a conversation that a company is likely to be reporting higher earnings this year. Both now issue research reports on the basis of the above. Which one of the following statements is *most appropriate*?

   A. Both Brown and Evans have breached Standards.

   B. Neither has breached Standards.

   C. Evans has breached Standards.

24. Which of the following *least accurately describes* Standard III.D – Performance Presentation?

    A. It requires members of CFA Institute to avoid misrepresentation of investment performance.

    B. It requires members of CFA Institute to adopt the Global Investment Presentation Standards.

    C. It relates to performance presentation and performance measurement.

25. The main purpose of Standard VI.C – Referral Fees, is to:

    A. Allow customers to reduce their costs by making referrals.

    B. Comply with the basic rule of fiduciary duties – the duty to disclose.

    C. Help the customer evaluate the full cost of services rendered.

26. Gail Faulkner is preparing a research report on a small biotech company for public distribution. Her supervisor sees a rough draft with favourable earnings projections. Faulkner later obtains revised data and lowers the favourable projections. Just before the report is published, Faulkner sees that her supervisor has substituted her earlier, more favourable projections in place of the less favourable projections. According to CFA Institute Code and Standards Faulkner should:

    A. Immediately report the incident to the regulatory authorities.

    B. Require either inclusion of the unfavourable earnings projections or removal of her name from the report.

    C. Request that the report include a disclaimer with respect to the earnings projections.

27. Lucy Miller is an analyst for the seafood industry. She has just received a package from the Lobster Shank, a company that is not one of her existing clients, containing 100 pounds of lobster tails; a delicacy. Miller estimates that the tails are worth over $8,000. According to the CFA Institute Code and Standards Miller should:

    A. Accept the gift, since it is from a company rather than a client.

    B. Refuse the gift because the Standards of Professional Conduct prohibit analysts from receiving gifts from the companies or industries they review.

    C. Return the gift, as it is a large gift from a company.

28. Vinzenca Sgarra, who has recently been promoted to senior analyst, with supervisory responsibilities and director of research at a regional brokerage firm, has been unable to implement a comprehensive compliance system. Given the lack of compliance system, what is Sgarra's *most appropriate* course of action?

    A. Avoid accepting supervisory responsibilities until reasonable procedures are adopted.

    B. Ignore the firm's policy and develop her own procedures.

    C. Resign from the firm.

29. Nedra Alexander is a financial analyst with ABC Brokerage Company. She is preparing a purchase recommendation on F & H Corporation. Which one of the following situations would *least likely* represent a conflict of interest that should be disclosed?

    A. Alexander is on retainer as a consultant to F & H Corporation.

    B. Alexander's brother-in-law is a supplier to F & H Corporation.

    C. ABC holds a substantial common stock position of F & H Corporation for its own account.

30. Martin Power heads the research department of a regional brokerage firm. The firm employs many analysts, some of whom are subject to the Code and Standards. Should Power delegate some of his supervisory duties, which statement *best* describes his responsibilities under CFA Institute Code and Standards?

    A. Power is released from responsibility for those duties delegated to his subordinates.

    B. Supervisory responsibility is retained by Power for all subordinates despite delegation of some of his duties.

    C. Power may not delegate supervisory duties to subordinates, because of the Code and Standards.

Progress Test 1 – Ethical and Professional Standards

Answers

1.   **C**   Maple can contact his old clients once he has left his old company provided he does not use his client lists to do so

See LOS 2a

2.   **B**   The charity is too small to be considered competition to her employer

See LOS 2a

3.   **C**   Standard VI.A Disclosure of Conflicts

See LOS 2a

4.   **B**   Standard III.C Suitability. Or when there is a material change in the investment recommendation given to a client

See LOS 2a

5.   **B**   Buying and selling securities for tax reasons, know as tax-loss harvesting, is allowed

See LOS 2a

6.   **C**   Standard II.A Material Nonpublic Information

See LOS 2a

7.   **C**   Standard II.A Material Nonpublic Information

See LOS 2a

8.   **A**   The GIPS standards are not explicitly incorporated in the Code of Ethics and Standards of Professional Conduct. However, members may rely on the standards to help ensure that they make no material misrepresentations regarding their performance

See LOS 4a

9.   **C**   Standard II.A – Material Nonpublic Information

See LOS 2a

10.   **A**   Verification is not mandatory. A firm may voluntarily hire an independent third party to verify their claim of compliance

See LOS 4b

11.   **B**   Standard VI.A – Disclosure of Conflicts

See LOS 2a

12.   **A**   Standard IV.A – Loyalty. Even though Long has no written contract he has an obligation to let Caspian act on the work he has done and should not disclose it to a prospective employer unless he obtains permission from Caspian to do so

See LOS 2a

13. **C** Yavy has failed in her supervisory role, not because her recommendation was acted upon as there were adequate procedures in place to prevent this, but because there were no procedures in place to review or record employee trading in a recommended stock

See LOS 2a

14. **B** Standard IV.A – Loyalty

See LOS 2a

15. **B** An objective is to ensure that performance data is accurate and consistent globally, not on a country by country basis

See LOS 4a

16. **C** Connor should base his recommendation on more information than a drilling estimate

See LOS 2a

17. **C** Standard II.A Material Nonpublic Information. Smith cannot trade or cause others to trade on the information unless it has been disseminated to the public

See LOS 2a

18. **B** Standard IV.C – Responsibilities of Supervisors. Checks should be carried out by supervisors

See LOS 2a

19. **C** Standard VII.B – Reference to the CFA Institute, the CFA Designation, and the CFA Program. Sanchez has implied a form of designation by giving himself this title

See LOS 2a

20. **C** Standard III.A – Loyalty, Prudence and Care. Since he believes that the directors' argument is a good one and the broker offers best execution and low commissions

See LOS 2a

21. **A**

See LOS 4c

22. **C** The rule of thumb is to follow the stricter of applicable legal requirements and the Code and Standards

See LOS 2a

23. **A** Standard V.A – Diligence and Reasonable Basis. A longer period of analysis would be required for Brown

See LOS 2a

24. **B** Adoption of the GIPS standards is the best way to ensure compliance although this is not obligatory

See LOS 2a

25. **C** According to Standard VI.C – Referral Fees, such disclosure will help the client evaluate any partiality shown in any recommendation of service and evaluate the full cost of the service

   See LOS 2a

26. **B** Standard I.D – Misconduct states that members shall not engage in any professional conduct involving dishonesty, fraud, deceit, or misrepresentation or commit any act that reflects adversely on their honesty, trustworthiness or professional competence. Faulkner should insist that the most recent, less favorable projections be included in the report

   See LOS 2a

27. **C** Standard I.B – Independence and Objectivity suggests modest gifts and entertainment are acceptable. Every member should avoid situations that might cause, or be perceived to cause, a loss of independence or objectivity in recommending investments or taking investment actions. Gifts from clients are less of a problem than gifts from a company

   See LOS 2a

28. **A** According to Standard IV.C – Responsibilities of Supervisors, a member with supervisory responsibility should bring an inadequate compliance system to the attention of the firm's senior managers and recommend corrective action. In the absence of a compliance system, and when it is clear they cannot carry out supervisory responsibilities, the member should decline in writing to accept supervisory responsibility

   See LOS 2a

29. **B** According to Standard VI.A – Disclosure of Conflicts, all potential conflicts of interest must be disclosed. The more obvious conflicts of interest are special relationships between a member and the member's firm or an issuer, underwriter or others with financial relationships, such as broker-dealer market-making activities, and positions involving material beneficial ownership of stock

   See LOS 2a

30. **B** Under Standard IV.C – Responsibilities of Supervisors, members may delegate supervisory duties to subordinates but delegation does not relieve them of their supervisory responsibilities. Any investment professionals with employees subject to their control or influence are considered to have supervisory responsibilities, and are required to take steps to prevent anyone under their supervision from violating the law or the Code and Standards

   See LOS 2a

STUDY GUIDANCE

Quantitative Methods: Basic Concepts

This guidance aims to identify the topics that we consider to be of premium importance for your exam preparation.

Study session 2 (Volume 1) comprises of:

Reading 5 The Time Value of Money

Reading 6 Discounted Cash Flow Applications

Reading 7 Statistical Concepts and Market Returns

Reading 8 Probability Concepts

Recommended study time is 19.5 hours of work.

 Exam focus

Quantitative Methods (study sessions 2 and 3) in total forms 12% of the examination. There will be 14-15 questions in each of the morning and afternoon papers. The questions will be split roughly 50% from study session 2 on basic concepts and 50% from study session 3 on application.

The exam focuses on your understanding of the concepts rather than your ability to do detailed mathematical calculations. It is likely that some of the questions will be factual, testing your knowledge of definitions or core knowledge of the concepts.

This is a key section as some of the concepts learnt are re-visited in other parts of the syllabus in different forms, e.g. discounted cash flow techniques are used in bond and equity valuation.

 Pre-requisites

Ability to use BA II calculator or other CFA approved calculator for time value of money calculations and other discounting functions.

Key areas

- Future value of single cash flows

- Compounding

- Present value of future cash flows

- Present value of annuities and perpetuities

- Present value of delayed cash flows including annuities and perpetuities

Content review – CFA curriculum

This chapter contains many example calculations. All of those mentioned in the 'key areas' section above are highly examinable. Elements of the examples often appear as questions within in the exam. The best advice for this section is to ensure that you are comfortable using the calculator and understand the appropriate terminology. To help understand how to enter the calculations into your calculator, BPP's calculator guide for the BAII Plus is a great resource as it shows step by step which buttons to press whilst working through the calculations.

Section 2 Interest Rates: Interpretation (pages 250-251)

The chapter starts with an interpretation of interest rates, and although less crucial, you should read this section trying to remember the definitions.

Section 3 The Future Value of a Single Cash Flow (pages 252-261)

This is the first key area and introduces the terminology which will be used throughout. It is important to understand this and make sure that you can replicate the calculations using your calculator. Examples 1 and 3 on pages 254 and 255 should be looked at and understood.

Section 3.1 The Frequency of Compounding

This section covers compounding and again is key. You must understand the relationship between different interest rates and the terminology. You should make sure you understand examples 4 and 5 on pages 257 and 258.

3 hours

Section 3.2 Continuous Compounding

You should read and understand this section especially the concept of what continuous compounding means but if you are struggling do not worry too much, it is not likely to be more than 1 question in the exam. Example 6 on page 259 is worth working through.

Section 3.3 Stated and Effective Rates

This is a key section in understanding compounding. What is important to appreciate is that you will generally be given the annual flat rate in questions, so if the compounding period is less than one year, you have to be able to deal with the implications for your calculations. Whilst there is no set example in the text, there is a worked calculation on pages 260-261 with a written explanation.

Section 4.1 Equal Cash Flows – Ordinary Annuity (pages 261-263)

This is an extension of Section 3 and covers the future value of multiple cash flows.

It is key to understand the concepts and calculations in order to value annuities. Make sure you understand example 7 on page 262.

Section 4.2 Unequal Cash Flows

Just read to confirm your understanding.

Section 5 The Present Value of a Single Cash Flow (pages 263-267)

It is likely that there will be more questions on present values than future values. Example 8 on page 264 and example 9 on page 265 cover the basic discounting of a cash flow. Example 10 on pages 266-267 incorporates both discounting future cash flows and the concept of compounding introduced in the previous section. This is a comprehensive example.

Section 6 The Present Value of a Series of Cash Flows (pages 267-275)

This covers the present value of multiple cash flows and the whole section is key. All examples should be worked through. These are examples 11 on page 268 and 12 on page 269. Example 13 on page 270 really brings together many of the concepts from this reading and it is unlikely that you will meet any more in depth calculations in the actual exam related to this section.

Sections 6.2 and 6.3 Perpetuities

These are particularly important sections as the concepts are applied to equity valuations later in the syllabus. It is worth looking over example 14 on page 272 and 15 on page 273 which cover these concepts well. Again, example 16, on page 274, brings together a number of concepts and is a good test of knowledge and understanding.

Section 7 Solving for Rates etc (pages 275-284)

This tests your understanding of the concepts by presenting the information in a different way. You can expect to be tested on your understanding of the concepts in the exam by having to solve for different parameters as well as discounted values. Examples 17-20 should be read and understood and can be found on pages 276 and 278 of the text. Example 21 on pages 279-280 is a fairly in depth calculation but has a good explanation of all the steps and is worth working through.

Sections 7.4 and 7.5

These need only be read quickly as they are lower priority and are more intuitive.

The chapter finishes with a summary on pages 284-5 which is a good revision aid followed by practice questions on page 286. Following the questions there are in-depth solutions starting on page 289 which are helpful to understand the methodology and technique employed.

Question practice

- It is recommended that you attempt practice questions 2 to 15 and 17 to 21 (pages 286-289).

- Students should make sure they understand the answers and take note of the answer techniques especially the time lines provided in the solutions.

- In addition, all questions in the BPP Question Bank should be attempted prior to the exam.

3 hours

Key areas

- Net Present Value (NPV) and Internal Rate of Return (IRR)
- Return measures
- Money market yields

Content review – CFA curriculum

1.5 hours

This chapter covers the use of discounting in financial investments and you can expect this to be examined in different forms in the exam.

Section 2.1 Net Present Value

This section covers the NPV and the NPV rule and although it may be intuitive, it should be read carefully especially the five steps noted in making calculations. Work through example 1 on page 308 and make sure you are happy with both parts.

Section 2.2 Internal Rate of Return

This section is a follow on from the NPV and once again should be read thoroughly including examples 2 and 3 on pages 309-310.

Section 2.3 Problems with the IRR Rule

This covers the very examinable area of problems with the IRR rule. It is important to understand the concept in order to be able to explain the problem as well as being able to do the calculations. Two worked examples are included in the text on page 312 and are worth reviewing.

Section 3 Portfolio Return Measurement

You must read these sections to understand the different measures and also understand the appropriateness of the measures. You are as likely to be asked a question about the concepts as you are to calculate any measures. Example 5 on page 318 covers both measures.

Section 4 Money Market Yields

The important thing is to learn the different yield definitions and to be able to convert one yield into another. Table 7 on page 323 is a good summary and example 7 on page 324 is very comprehensive.

The summary section at the end of the chapter on page 325 also reminds you of the measures as well as the key points covered within the chapter. This is a good revision guide. You may wish to leave this section until later, where you will be focusing on other bond yield measures.

Question practice

1 hour

- You should at least attempt questions 1 to 6 starting on page 327 for all round practice making sure you understand all the answers which follow on page 330.

STUDY SESSION 2 – READING 7

Statistical Concepts and Market Returns (page 335)

5 hours

Key areas

- Summarising data
- Data presentation
- Measures of central tendency (averages)
- Measures of dispersion (variance/deviation)
- Symmetry and skewness

Content review – CFA curriculum

Section 2 Fundamental Concepts (pages 336-339)

This is likely to be examined but not in detail.

Sections 2.1 and 2.2 need to be read through, focusing on the definitions given in bold.

Section 2.3 Measurement Scales

Focus on the basic definitions and the order of the scales. There always tends to be a question requiring you to distinguish between nominal, ordinal, interval and ratio scales.

Section 3 Frequency Distributions (pages 339-348)

Again, focus on the definitions and only the basic calculations up to the cumulative relative frequency at the end of page 343. It is not necessary to look at the remaining part of this section; it is just an overly complex example.

Section 4 Graphic Presentation of Data (pages 348-352)

Read through quickly. You need only focus on the two definitions of the histogram and polygon.

Section 5 Measures of Central Tendency (pages 352-370)

3 hours

This section covers different measures of averages. It is important to read and understand the definitions, concepts, properties and why different measures are better / worse in different circumstances. If you understand the calculations easily it is of less important to work through the examples which are far more detailed than you will see in the exam. Remember the geometric mean is always less than the arithmetic mean (unless all numbers in the set are the same) so if you have a question in the exam around this and you forget the formula, as long as you know the arithmetic mean you know the geometric mean is less than this which may help to eliminate all but the correct answer.

Section 6 Other Measures of Location (pages 370-376)

Low priority and it is only really necessary to read the first paragraph.

Section 7 Measures of Dispersion (pages 376-394)

This is an area where a number of students struggle but the key thing is to be able to understand the concepts and the simple formulas. You will not have to make large complex calculations in the exam.

Section 7.1 The Range

You should read and learn the definitions of dispersion and range in the introduction on page 376.

Section 7.2 The Mean Absolute Deviation (MAD)

This should be read carefully making sure you understand the terminology. This is crucial for the sections which follow. If you understand the formula for mean absolute deviation, it is not necessary to go though the example on pages 377-8 in detail.

Section 7.3 Population Variance and Population Standard Deviation

This is key area and you should learn the formulas for variance and standard deviation as well as the concepts of what they represent. Example 11 on page 380 is a way of showing how the formulas work in practice.

Section 7.4 Sample Variance and Standard Deviation

This is also a key section and you need to understand the relationship between samples and the overall population. You need to learn the formulae for samples and recognize how they differ from formulae for a whole population. Example 12 on page 382 is arguably too detailed to be useful and it is not necessary to go through this or tables 21 and 22.

Section 7.5 Semivariance

Should be read through quickly but is not considered key.

Section 7.6 Chebyshev's Inequality

This frequently comes up in exams and it is well worth reading this section fully. It is also a useful revision guide as in order to understand it you need to remember about distributions and standard deviations learnt in previous sections. Example 13 on page 387 is not necessary to go through in detail.

Sections 7.7 and 7.8 Coefficient of Variation and Sharpe Ratio

It is necessary to learn the formulas and in basic terms what they represent but not necessary to go into the descriptive detail. The Sharpe ratio is often examined and pops up again in both Level II and Level III studies. The Sharpe ratio will be covered in Study Session 12.

Sections 8 and 9 Symmetry, Skewness and Kurtosis (pages 394-403)

The key things are to understand the characteristics of a normal distribution and what is meant by skew and kurtosis. Do not learn the formulas and it is not necessary to go through the examples.

Section 10 Using Means (pages 403-405)

Non-key.

The summary goes through the key points and is a very useful revision guide.

Question practice

- The chapter summary on page 405 is a useful revision aid. There are a lot of practice problems in this chapter. It is recommended that you focus on questions 16 to 18 on page 413 and questions 20 to 25 on pages 414-5.

- Especially for the conceptual questions, make sure you understand any questions you have not got right. In the problems requiring detailed calculations the key is knowing what calculations you need to make rather than actually making all the detailed calculations in themselves.

2 hours

- In addition, the BPP Question Bank questions should be attempted prior to the exam.

STUDY SESSION 2 – READING 8

Probability Concepts (page 431)

6 hours

Key areas

- Probability expected value

- Combining events and conditional probability

- Bayes formula and probability trees

Content review – CFA curriculum

This chapter provides an introduction to probability and the underlying core concepts. It extends to correlation and covariance which is an important part of portfolio management. It details the required formulas and methodologies for working out different sorts of probability problems. As well as the numerical aspects you should seek to understand the concepts and definitions.

Section 2 Probability, Expected Value and Variance (pages 432-454)

This section is the introduction to different sorts of events and definitions of probabilities. It contains a number of definitions which are important to learn. You should read through the whole section.

It is important to familiarise yourself with the terminology, the notation and the way probability values are stated.

The multiplication and addition rules for probabilities are key. Figure 1 and example 3 on page 440 are important aids to understanding the addition rule.

Examples 4 on page 441 and 6 on page 443 are also good to work through. Example 7 on pages 444-5 and question 2 is also worth trying to calculate the answer before looking at the solution.

Example 8 on page 446 covers expected value and this is an area which is often examined and an application comes later in Corporate Finance, so it is worth making sure you understand this fully.

4 hours

Figure 2 on page 449 re-enforces the concept of the total probability rule for expected value and it is a good way to visualise this important concept. If you can then work through example 10 on page 451 successfully generating the answers without looking at the solutions, this will demonstrate that you have a good understanding of basic probability calculations.

Example 11 does not have to be worked through.

Section 3 Portfolio Expected Return and Variance of Return (pages 454-462)

Portfolio variance is a key part of modern portfolio theory and this section introduces the idea. For the exam it is necessary to know how to calculate the portfolio expected values and returns, the definition of covariance and the definition of correlation. You would not be expected to do any detailed calculations in the exam and it should be of very low priority to go into the detail of covariance matrices shown in the text. In example 12 on page 460, it is worth working through question 1.

Section 4 Topics in Probability (pages 462-470)

The key parts of this section are Bayes formula and the principles of counting, although the text does over complicate Bayes.

Principles of counting should be read and the principles understood. These calculations can be made easily on your calculators and as well as learning the formulas you should learn how to use your calculator for this.

The summary at the end beginning of page 470 is a useful revision guide and should be gone through before attempting the practice problems.

Question practice

- Practice problems can be found from page 473 onwards and questions 5-8 and 17, 19 and 20 will test your all round knowledge of the key areas.

2 hours

- In addition, all questions in the BPP Question Bank should be attempted prior to the exam.

STUDY GUIDANCE

Quantitative Methods: Application

This guidance aims to identify the topics that we consider to be of premium importance for your exam preparation.

Study session 3 (Volume 1) comprises of:

Reading 9   Common Probability Distributions

Reading 10   Sampling and Estimation

Reading 11   Hypothesis Testing

Reading 12   Technical Analysis

Recommended study time is 19 hours of work. An additional 2 hours should be added to complete Progress Test 2.

 ## Exam focus

Quantitative Methods (study sessions 2 and 3) in total forms 12% of the examination. There will be 14 - 15 questions in each of the morning and afternoon papers.

A lot of students struggle with some of the calculations but the focus of the exam is on your understanding of the concepts rather than your ability to do detailed mathematical calculations. It is likely that some of the questions will be factual, testing your knowledge of definitions or core knowledge of the concepts. Do not fall into the trap of thinking that the exam will be focusing on the complicated areas at the end of hypothesis testing (Reading 11) – this will absolutely not be the case.

 ## Pre-requisites

You should have covered study session 2, Readings 5 - 8 before attempting this section.

Key areas

- Binomial distribution
- The normal distribution
- Application of the normal distribution

Content review – CFA curriculum

Section 1 Introduction and Discrete Random Variables (page 488)

You should read through this section briefly noting the definitions of the variables/functions in bold.

Section 2.1 Discrete Uniform Distribution (page 490)

Only requires a quick read through.

Section 2.2 Binomial Distribution (page 492)

Reference is made in this section to equity options but this will be covered in more detail in the derivatives section.

This section is key as there are a number of different elements within it which are regularly tested in the exam. Work through examples 2-4 on pages 492-7 but example 5 is less crucial if you have understood the concepts and calculations up to this point. Remember from Reading 8 that a number of combinations can be calculated on your calculator without having to remember the formulas.

Table 4 on page 499 is very worthwhile trying to learn. This can be an easy mark or two in the exam and you can save yourself time by remembering the formulas. Example 6 on page 499 is useful but after this the remaining text need only be glanced over.

3 hours

Section 3 Continuous Random Variables (page 501)

It is necessary to understand what this is but not necessary to go into the mathematical detail or to work through example 7.

Section 3.2 The Normal Distribution

It is key to understand the base properties of the normal distribution. There are some elements of the distribution that you need to remember but you will not have to learn detailed statistical tables or the most complex mathematical formulae. In the exam, exerts from the tables will be given to you as part of the question.

Look at the graphs in figure 5 on page 505 and understand the different distributions. Do not bother at all with the mathematical formula for the distribution, it is not examinable.

The next stage is absolutely key, regarding standard normal distributions and standardising.

You do not have to memorise the data in table 5 but you should understand what it is telling you. Do look to remember the most frequently reference values noted (90th, 95th and 99th percentiles). Learning these will, at a minimum, save you time in the exam and it is possible you may be asked a direct question requiring you to remember a key percentile.

In example 8 on page 510, work through questions 1 and 2 but you need not do question 3.

Section 3.3 Applications of the Normal Distribution

This section primarily covers safety first rules. This is frequently examined and this section also reinforces the principles and concepts learnt previously. Work through example 9 on page 512 which provides comprehensive coverage of potential areas of examination.

Sections 3.4 and Section 4 Lognormal Distribution and Monte Carlo Analysis and Historical Simulation

Beyond knowing what these are used for and why, these sections are non-key and need not be read in detail.

As before, the summary starting on page 525 is a useful revision guide.

Question practice

- Distribution tables can be found at the back of the book in Appendix A (page 695). You will need these in order to answer the problems.

2 hours

- Problems 11 to 14 (page 530) and 19 and 20 (page 532) are considered highest priority.

Key areas

- Sampling theory
- Distribution of sample mean
- Confidence intervals
- Students T distribution
- Other issues in sampling

A number of students struggle to master this section. If you are struggling with the mathematical side of it, focus on understanding the concepts rather than the detailed applications.

It is necessary to understand the concepts in this chapter before undertaking Reading 11.

Content review – CFA curriculum

The reading explores how sampling is used to estimate the characteristics of the populations as a whole.

Section 2 Sampling (page 540)

Make sure you read and understand the three definitions given in bold of simple random samples, sampling error and sampling distribution on page 541.

Section 2.2 Stratified Random Sampling

You need to understand the definition and the concept of indexing but you do not have to work through the example.

Section 2.3 Time-Series and Cross Sectional Data

It is only necessary to understand what is meant by this and you do not have to work the example.

Section 3 Distribution of the Sample Mean (page 546)

Section 3.1 Central Limit Theorem

3 hours

This section is key and you must understand the concept and the definition of the standard error of the sample mean. Look at the example given in the slides and try to understand this which also covers confidence intervals (section 4.2). The exam will either test your factual understanding of the concepts or ask a question along the lines of those found in the BPP Question Bank.

Section 4 Point and Interval Estimates of the Population Mean (page 549)

Section 4.1 Point Estimators

Just focus on the three definitions given in this section, unbiasedness, efficiency, and consistency.

Section 4.2 Confidence Intervals for the Population Mean

This is also a key section.

Seek to understand how to construct confidence intervals, confidence intervals for the population mean and the reliability factors. Example 4 on page 553 is quite short and if you can understand this you will know all you need to know on this topic.

You must then also understand what is meant by degrees of freedom and the T statistic or T distribution and when to use it.

Example 5 on page 556 is similar to example 4.

Section 4.3 Selection of Sample Size

Just understand the relationship between sample sizes and confidence intervals. It is not necessary to go through example 6.

Section 5 More on Sampling (page 559)

There are four sub-sections on various sampling bias. It is only necessary to understand what is meant by the terms. You do not need to read all the detail but it is worth reading the answer in example 7 on page 564.

The summary starting on page 565 is a good revision guide and if you feel as if you know and understand most of what is covered in the summary you can feel confident about this section.

Question practice

- Attempt practice problems 3, 5, 6 on page 567 and 21 to 22 on page 570 for closest to exam style questions.

  1 hour

- In addition, all questions in the BPP Question Bank should be attempted prior to the exam.

Key areas

- Role of hypothesis testing
- Approach to hypothesis testing
- Types of hypothesis

As in Reading 10, a number of students struggle with some of the calculations. Focus on understanding the concepts. In the exam, the CFA will more likely examine your understanding of the concepts rather than your ability to apply them.

Content review – CFA curriculum

Section 1 Introduction (page 578)

Just a quick overview is needed.

Section 2 Hypothesis Testing (pages 579-588)

Read through this section thoroughly, at least up to the section defining the power of a test. It covers most of the necessary core definitions and core concepts. This is probably the key part of this reading.

Even if you have understood all the concepts so far in this chapter, there is probably limited value in reading through completely what is a very detailed description and analysis in the book.

You should finish reading section 2.

Section 3.1 Tests Concerning a Single Mean (page 588)

Read the first part of section 3.1, tests concerning a single mean, but do not go through the examples. It is not necessary either to go through the z-test alternative section.

Section 3.2 Tests Concerning Differences Between Means (page 596)   **4 hours**

Read through the text but you do not need to go through the examples.

Section 3.3 Tests Concerning Mean Differences (page 600)

Just read up to equation 13 on page 601. There is no need to go through the large table 5 or example 6.

Section 4.1 Hypothesis Testing Concerning a Single Variance (page 604)

Read through and look at example 7 on page 605.

Section 4.2 Tests Concerning the Equality of Two Variances (page 606)

Read the text and but there is no need to go through the examples.

Section 5 Other Issues: Non-parametric Inference (page 609)

This is non key section and can just be glanced over. The summary section that follows on page 614 contains everything you will need to know on this in the last three points.

If you are clear and feel you have understood the section aside from the last three points it is suggested that you do not spend much time on the summary section. Instead use it as a reference guide if there are practice problems you cannot do. It will be useful later as a revision guide closer to the exam.

Question practice

- Question 1 on page 617 serves as a good refresher of key terms - refer to the summary if necessary.

- Attempt questions 3 (page 617), 5-9 (pages 618-9), 16 and 17 (pages 621-2).

2 hours

- In addition, all questions in the BPP Question Bank should be attempted prior to the exam.

Key areas

- What is technical analysis?

- Advantages

- Major sorts of technical analysis

This is not a topic which is likely to be examined extensively.

Content review – CFA curriculum

It is not necessary in our view to read through this chapter in full. If instead you read the summary section at the end beginning at the bottom of page 683 you will probably cover everything you need to know and some of it is intuitive. If you do not understand something in the summary you could refer to the main text for that specific point.

2 hours

Question practice

- Practice problems 1-28 (pages 686-689) all follow the exam format and cover extensively all areas of the reading. Attempting these questions having read the summary section will give you a complete coverage. You may want to save some questions for revision practice later on.

2 hours

- In addition, all questions in the BPP Question Bank should be attempted prior to the exam.

CHECKPOINT – END OF STUDY SESSIONS 2 AND 3

You are now able to attempt the **Progress Test 2 on Quantitative Methods**.

2 hours

NOTES

Progress Test 2 – Quantitative Methods

Questions

1. Consider the following series of year-end cash flows.

   Year 1   −$15,000
   Year 2 $6,000
   Year 3 $10,000
   Year 4 $1,000

   Which of the following best represents the internal rate of return of the cash flows, and assuming a discount rate of 10%, which is *closest* to the terminal value of the cash flows at the end of Year 4?

	IRR	VALUE AT END OF YEAR 4
A.	6.77%	$26,791
B.	6.77%	−$705
C.	7.67%	−$705

2. An investor wishes to receive an annual payment of $10,000 at the end of each year from an annuity for ten years with the first payment ten years from now. Assuming that the annual rate of return will be 8%, the amount of money that needs to be put on deposit now to achieve this annual payment rate is *closest to*:

   A. $31,080.

   B. $33,570.

   C. $67,100.

3. The following information is available about the returns on two stocks.

Probability	Return from Stock A	Return from Stock B
0.5	10%	8%
0.2	-4%	2%
0.3	13%	10%

   The expected return from a portfolio consisting of 75% in Stock A and 25% in Stock B will be *closest to*:

   A. 6.3%.

   B. 6.4%.

   C. 7.9%.

4. An event has a probability of 0.2 of arising. Which of the following would be the odds against the event that would be offered in a wager such that the expected value of the wager would be zero?

    A. 3

    B. 4

    C. 5

5. David Walker is evaluating for his client four alternative investments with the following characteristics.

	Expected Return	Standard Deviation of Returns
Investment A	10%	8%
Investment B	15%	12%
Investment C	20%	16%

    The client has a minimum required return of 2%. Assuming returns are normally distributed, the investment that is *most appropriate* for your client, according to Roy's safety-first criterion is:

    A. Investment A.

    B. Investment B.

    C. Investment C.

6. When interpreting a candlestick chart, which of the following best explains the occurrence of a long unshaded candle body that is a similar length to its vertical line?

    A. The stock closed higher than it opened on the day and volatility was significant.

    B. The stock closed lower than it opened on the day and volatility was very low.

    C. The stock closed higher than it opened on the day and volatility was very low.

7. A sample of 100 items has a mean of 60 and the standard error is 5. The confidence interval of the mean of the population using a confidence level of 95% is *closest to*:

    Probability in one tail

Degrees of freedom	0.100	0.050	0.025	0.010	0.005
∞	1.282	1.645	1.960	2.326	2.576

    A. 55 to 65.

    B. 45 to 75.

    C. 50 to 70.

8. A sample of 20 items has a mean of 92 and a standard error of 10. The 90% confidence interval of the population mean T is *closest to*:

Extract from Student's *t*-distribution.

Degrees of Freedom	Probability				
	0.1	0.05	0.025	0.01	0.005
18	1.33	1.73	2.10	2.55	2.88
19	1.32	1.72	2.09	2.54	2.86
20	1.31	1.71	2.08	2.53	2.84
21	1.30	1.70	2.07	2.52	2.83

A. 74.9 to 109.1.

B. 74.8 to 109.2.

C. 78.8 to 105.2.

9. In hypothesis testing, a Type I error is:

A. Rejecting the null hypothesis when it is false.

B. Rejecting the null hypothesis when it is true.

C. Failing to reject the null hypothesis when it is false.

10. List the following funds in order of risk-adjusted performance (best to worst) using the Sharpe ratio. The risk-free return over the same period was 3%.

Fund	Return	Standard Deviation of Returns
I	9%	11%
II	12%	15%
III	19%	20%
IV	22%	30%

A. III, IV, II, I

B. I, II, IV, III

C. IV, III, II, I

11. An investment of $231 will increase in value to $268 in three years. If continuous compounding is used, the stated interest rate is *closest to*:

A. 3.0%.

B. 4.0%.

C. 5.0%.

12. An investor has gathered the following return expectations for Stocks X and Y.

	Bear Market	Normal Market	Bull Market
Probability	0.2	0.5	0.3
Stock X	–20%	18%	50%
Stock Y	–15%	20%	10%

The expected return for Stock X, and the standard deviation of returns on Stock Y is *closest to*:

	STOCK X EXPECTED RETURN	STOCK Y STANDARD DEVIATION
A.	18%	13%
B.	18%	8%
C.	20%	13%

13. The table shows the annual rate of return for JSI's common stock.

	2008	2009	2010	2011
Return	14%	19%	–10%	14%

The geometric mean rate of return and the median rate of return for JSI's common stock over the four years is *closest to*:

	GEOMETRIC MEAN	MEDIAN RATE
A.	8.62%	4.5%
B.	9.25 %	14%
C.	8.62%	14%

14. Which one of the following statements is *least likely* to be an example of a nonparametric test?

A. Testing the variance of a population.

B. Analyzing data that has been gathered in the form of ordinal data.

C. Ascertaining if a data series is random through time.

15. A loan has a fixed rate of interest of 8%, compounded quarterly. What would be outstanding on a loan of $1,000 after 10 years, if in that time no repayments were made.

The outstanding balance would be closest to:

A. $1,800

B. $2,159

C. $2,208

16. An individual retiring today has the choice between an immediate lump sum of $900,000 or an annuity with 20 payments of $70,000 per year with the first payment being made today. Which of the following statements is *most accurate* if the appropriate discount rate for the annuity is 5.5%?

    A. The individual should choose the lump sum because its present value is $87,464 higher.

    B. The individual should choose the lump sum because its present value is $17,464 higher.

    C. The individual should choose the annuity because its present value is $6,527 higher.

17. Which one of the following statements is *most accurate* regarding the central limit theorem?

    A. A normally distributed population will have a distribution of sample means that is normally distributed with a mean of μ and a standard deviation of $s \div \sqrt{n}$ where s is the standard deviation of a sample.

    B. Any large population will be normally distributed.

    C. A large population will have a distribution of sample means that will be approximately normally distributed, provided the sample size is at least 30 items.

18. A quantitative model aims to identify stocks that will experience growth in profits over the year. The model correctly identifies 60% of the companies that experience a growth in profits as such. It also identifies 20% of companies that do not experience growth in profits as likely to have profit growth. 40% of companies are expected to experience profit growth overall.

    The model has identified a stock as likely to experience profit growth. Using Bayes' theorem, the posterior probability that the stock will experience profit growth is *closest to*:

    A. 12%.

    B. 24%.

    C. 67%.

19. The variance of a sample of people's height was 8, and that of shoe size was 12. If the covariance between the two samples is calculated to be 5.7, the correlation coefficient is *closest to*:

    A. 0.0594.

    B. 0.2437.

    C. 0.5818.

20. The following table gives details of the conditional probability of event A arising in two different scenarios, given that the scenario has occurred.

Scenario	Probability of the Scenario Arising	Conditional Probability of Event A Arising
I	0.7	0.3
II	0.3	0.6

    Which of the following is *closest to* the total probability of event A arising?

    A. 0.9.

    B. Greater than 0.39 but less than 0.9.

    C. 0.39.

21. If a distribution has fatter tails than the normal distributions, then it is:

    A. Leptokurtic.

    B. Negatively skewed.

    C. Platykurtic.

22. The probability distribution of annual returns from investing in a company is given below.

Return p.a.	Probability
7%	0.2
8%	0.4
9%	0.2
10%	0.2

    The mean and standard deviation of the annual rates of return on this investment are *closest to*:

	MEAN	STANDARD DEVIATION
A.	8.4%	1.04%
B.	8.4%	1.02%
C.	8.5%	1.12%

23. With respect to Bayes' theorem, which of the following equations is used to calculate the posterior probability of an event?

    A. $\dfrac{\text{Probability of the event given new information}}{\text{Unconditional probability of the event}} \times \text{Prior probability of the event}$

    B. $\dfrac{\text{Probability of new information given the event}}{\text{Unconditional probability of the new information}} \times \text{Prior probability of the event}$

    C. $\dfrac{\text{Probability of the event given new information}}{\text{Unconditional probability of the event}} \times \text{Prior probability of the information}$

24. Which one of the following is *least* likely to be a characteristic of Elliot Wave Theory?

    A. Elliot Wave Theory can be applied in both very short-term trading and very long-term analysis.

    B. The longest of the waves within the Elliot Wave Theory is called the 'grand supercycle'.

    C. The numbers in the Fibonacci sequence represent the number of waves in each of Elliot's cycle pattern.

25. Which of the following is an example of an ordinal scale?

    A. Temperature in Celsius.

    B. Beta factor.

    C. Assigning numerical values to credit ratings.

26. An investment of $335 grows to $546 over a period of four years. The annual compound growth rate is *closest to*:

A. 11%.

B. 12%.

C. 13%.

 27. Which of the following *best describes* a major limitation of Monte Carlo simulation?

A. It only provides statistical estimates.

B. It cannot be used for sensitivity analysis.

C. It cannot be used in the calculation of value at risk (VAR).

 28. Which one of the following is the *most appropriate* construction of the null and alternative hypothesis for a one-tailed test?

	NULL HYPOTHESIS	ALTERNATIVE HYPOTHESIS
A.	$\mu = \mu_0$	$\mu \geq \mu_0$
B.	$\mu = \mu_0$	$\mu > \mu_0$
C.	$\mu \geq \mu_0$	$\mu < \mu_0$

29. The probability of a share price going up on any one day is 60%. The share price can either go up or down. If a share price is analyzed over ten days and the share price movement is deemed to be independent across days, the variance of the share price movement is *closest to*:

A. 1.55.

B. 2.40.

C. 4.00.

30. If the sample variance of a stock is 22 and the sample mean is 4, the coefficient of variation is *closest to*:

A. 0.18.

B. 0.85.

C. 1.17.

Progress Test 2 – Quantitative Methods

Answers

1. **C** The IRR of 7.67% can be obtained by using your calculator, using the following cash flows.

Time	Cash Flow
0	–
1	–15,000
2	6,000
3	10,000
4	1,000

Using the same cash flows and a discount rate of 10%, the present value of the cash flows is –481.5.

Using the relationship between present values and future values, the value of the cash flow at the end of the Year 4 is given by

$-481.5 \times 1.1^4 = -705$

Alternatively, if you have the Texas BA11 Plus Professional, you can compute NFV, which is one arrow on from NPV

See LOS 6a and 5e

2. **B** PMT $= 10,000$

N $= 10$

I/Y $= 8$

CPT PY $= 67,101$

Discount back 9 years as this is the value of an annuity where the first payment is at time 10, hence we are valuing it at time 9.

Amount to be deposited now $= 67,101 \times \dfrac{1}{1.08^9} = 33,567$ (rounded up to 33,570)

Alternatively, use your cash flow function

CF0 = 0

C01 = 0, Fo1 = 9

CO2 = 10,000, FO2 = 10

CPT NPV

See LOS 5e

3. **C** Expected return of A = 0.5 × 10% + 0.2 × (–4%) + 0.3 × 13% = 8.1%

Expected return of B = 0.5 × 8% + 0.2 × 2% + 0.3 × 10% = 7.4%

Expected return from a portfolio consisting of 75% in stock A and 25% in stock B = 0.75 × 8.1% + 0.25 × 7.4% = 7.9%

See LOS 8l

4. **B** Odds against an event = $\dfrac{1-P(E)}{P(E)} = \dfrac{0.8}{0.2} = 4$

See LOS 8c

5. **C**

Investment	Safety First Ratio (E(R) - $R_{minimum}$)/ σ
A	(10%-2%)/8% = 1.000
B	(15%-2%)/12% = 1.083
C	(20% - 2%)/16% = 1.125

C is the best alternative as it has the largest safety first ratio

See LOS 9n

6. **A** The candle has two elements, the vertical line and the body of the candle. The vertical line represents the range of the security price in the day. Therefore a long line represents high volatility. A shaded body represents a security that closed lower than the opening price on the day. An unshaded body represents a security that closed higher than the opening price on the day

See LOS 12b

7. **C** Since sample size is very large, the Student's t-distribution approximates to the normal distribution

$\bar{x} \pm 1.96 \times SE$

$= 60 \pm 1.96 \times 5$

i.e. from 50 to 70

See LOS 9m

8. **B** 19 degrees of freedom, 5% probability (two-tailed 90%)

$92 \pm 1.72 \times 10 = 74.8$ to 109.2

See LOS 9m

9. **B** This will arise when the sample mean lies in the rejection area above the critical value

See LOS 11b

10. **A** Sharpe ratio = $\dfrac{r_p - r_f}{\sigma_p}$

I $\dfrac{9-3}{11} = 0.545$

II $\dfrac{12-3}{15} = 0.600$

III $\dfrac{19-3}{20} = 0.8$

IV $\dfrac{22-3}{30} = 0.633$

Higher Sharpe measures are desirable since we are generating a greater amount of excess return per unit of risk that we are taking

See LOS 7i

11. **C** $231e^{3r} = 268$

$$e^{3r} = \frac{268}{231} = 1.1602$$

$3r = LN\ 1.1602$

$3r = 0.1486$

$r = 0.0495 = 4.95\%$

See LOS 5c and d

12. **C** The formula for the expected return is

Stock X: E(R) = 0.2(–20%) + 0.5(18%) + 0.3(50%)

= –4% + 9% + 15%

= 20%

Stock Y: E(R) = 0.2(–15%) + 0.5(20%) + 0.3(10%)

= –3% + 10% + 3%

= 10%

$$\sigma = \sqrt{0.2 \times \left(-25^2\right) + 0.5 \times 10^2 + 0.3 \times 0}$$

$\sigma = 13.23\%$

See LOS 8l

13. **C** $r = (1.14 \times 1.19 \times 0.90 \times 1.14)^{1/4} - 1$

$= (1.392)^{1/4} - 1$

$= 1.0862 - 1$

$= 0.0862$ or 8.62%

The median is the middle ranking item, 14%

See LOS 7e

14. **A** The variance is a parameter. Nonparametric tests are appropriate when we are testing a quantity other than a parameter (e.g. if a data series is random through time) or when we are not making the restrictive assumptions present in a parametric test

See LOS 11j

15. **C** The interest rate to apply is 2% for 40 periods

$1,000 \times 1.02^{40} = 2,208$

Remember that interest rates are quoted on a flat basis for the full year

See LOS 5c

16. **B** The annuity is equivalent to a 19-year ordinary annuity and $70,000 paid today

Present value of annuity = 812,536 (using calculator cash flow function) + 70,000 = 882,536

Present value of lump sum = 900,000 (17,464 higher)

See LOS 5e

17. **C** The distribution of sample means will only be Normally distributed if we use the standard deviation of the population to calculate the standard error, otherwise they will follow the t-distribution.

Large populations will only be approximately Normally distributed

See LOS 10e

18. **C** Using a tree

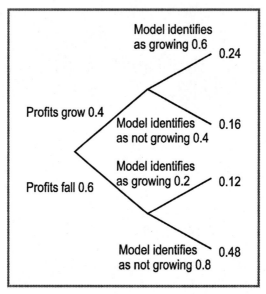

Given that a stock has been identified as likely to have profit growth, the probability of it having profit growth is 0.24 ÷ (0.24 + 0.12) = 0.67

Using the Bayes Theorem formula:

Probability of new information given the event (i.e. the probability that a stock will be identified as profit growth, given that it does have profit growth) = 0.6

Unconditional probability of the new information (i.e. the probability that the model will identify a stock as profit growth): 0.4 × 0.6 + 0.6 × 0.2 = 0.36

Prior probability that a stock will give profit growth: 0.4

Posterior probability: $\dfrac{0.6}{0.36} \times 0.4 = 0.67$

See LOS 8n

19. **C** $\mathrm{Cor}_{ab} = \dfrac{\mathrm{Cov}_{ab}}{\sigma_a \sigma_b} = \dfrac{5.7}{\sqrt{8}\sqrt{12}}$

See LOS 8k

20. **C** Scenarios I and II add up to a total probability of 1, suggesting that they are exclusive and exhaustive. The total probability of A is therefore 0.7 × 0.3 + 0.3 × 0.6 = 0.39

See LOS 8f

21. **A**   Analysts should always be careful of leptokurtic distributions, as it means that extreme events occur more than would be expected if the world was normally distributed. This is often the case in financial markets

See LOS 7l

22. **B**

p	r	pr	$(r - \bar{r})$	$p(r - \bar{r})^2$
0.2	7	1.4	-1.4	0.392
0.4	8	3.2	-0.4	0.064
0.2	9	1.8	0.6	0.072
0.2	10	2.0	1.6	0.512
	$\bar{r} =$	8.4		1.040

$$\sigma = \sqrt{1.04} = 1.020\%$$

See LOS 8l

23. **B**   Posterior probability is the revised probability based on additional new information

See LOS 8n

24. **C**   The relationship between the *heights* of waves are described by Fibonacci ratios, not the *number* of waves in each cycle pattern.

If you did not know the answer to this question at least you can use questions like this to learn from, i.e. what the Elliot Wave Theory is used for. You are likely to see only a question or two on technical analysis

See LOS 12g

25. **C**   Ordinal scales reflect the order of values (credit riskiness) but there is no numerical meaning in the actual number other than its ranking in a sequence. Temperature in Celsius and a beta factor are examples of interval scales as the difference between scale values are equal

See LOS 7a

26. **C** $4\sqrt{\dfrac{546}{335}} - 1 = 0.1299$

See LOS 5d

27. **A**   It is difficult to do sensitivity analysis for historical simulation

See LOS 9q

28. **C**   Remember that the hypotheses should over all possible outcomes and the null hypothesis should also contain the 'is equal to' sign. Note that B is an abbreviation on the hypotheses and C is the better answer

See LOS 11a

29.   **B**   This is a binomial problem

Variance = $np(1-p) = 10 \times 0.6 \times 0.4 = 2.4$

See LOS 9f

30.   **C**   Coefficient of variation = $\dfrac{S}{\bar{X}} = \dfrac{\sqrt{22}}{4} = 1.17$

See LOS 7i

STUDY GUIDANCE

Economics: Microeconomic Analysis

This guidance aims to identify the topics that we consider to be of premium importance for your exam preparation.

Study session 4 (Volume 2) comprises of:

Reading 13   Demand and Supply Analysis: Introduction

Reading 14   Demand and Supply Analysis: Consumer Demand

Reading 15   Demand and Supply Analysis: The Firm

Reading 16   The Firm and Market Structures

Recommended study time is 17 hours of work.

 ## Exam focus

Economics represents 10% of the exam and is covered in three study sessions (4, 5 and 6). This study session is likely to represent approximately 3 - 4% of the exam. There is a lot of material for a relatively small percentage of the exam and it is important therefore to focus on the key points which are more likely to be examined. These are highlighted within the online lectures, which you should watch if you are short of study time as it will save you time wasted on areas that are not high priority. You are not expected to be an economist and the examination only tests your understanding of a few core areas within economics.

 ## Pre-requisites

There are no pre-requisites to this study session.

Key areas

- Principles of demand and supply
- Market equilibrium and how it is achieved
- Demand elasticities

Content review – CFA curriculum

2 hours

This reading provides an excellent overview of basic principles and concepts of microeconomics. The latter section covers elasticity of demand which is a core concept in economics and one you must learn if you are to understand the rest of the syllabus. It is almost certain that some sort of question(s) will come up on this topic.

Section 2 Types of Market (pages 7-8)

Have a quick read through this first section and be able to distinguish between a factor market and a goods market. Complete the two questions in example 1 on page 8 as these are a good indication of exactly how this section could be tested in the real exam.

Section 3.1 and 3.2 The Demand Function and the Demand Curve, and Changes in Demand v Movement along the Demand Curve (pages 9-12)

Go through these two sections carefully, using the graphs on pages 11 and 12 to aide your understanding. Make sure you can distinguish between a movement along a demand curve and a shift in a demand curve. Work through example 2 on page 12 as a good summary to these sections.

Sections 3.3 and 3.4 The Supply Function and the Supply Curve, and Changes in the Supply Curve v Movement along the Supply Curve (pages 13-16)

As with the demand curve, use the graphs on pages 14 and 15 and work through example 3 on page 16 which summarises the key points made about the supply curve.

Section 3.5 Aggregating the Demand and Supply Functions (page 17-20)

The natural step from individual demand and supply curves is to now aggregate and represent the demand and supply of a whole market. Work through example 4 on page 18 and if you are happy, no need to go through example 5 on page 19 as this just repeats the same concept.

Sections 3.6 and 3.7 Market Equilibrium, and the Market Mechanism (pages 20-27)

Work through all the graphs in this section (pages 20, 23, 25 and 26), making sure you are able to understand how an equilibrium price is arrived at. Also, be able to explain both a stable and unstable equilibrium with real life examples.

Section 3.8 Auctions as a Way to Find an Equilibrium Price (pages 27-30)

Focus on the definitions in bold for this section. Work through example 8 on page 30 and understand how the winning bid is arrived at. You will not be presented with something this long in an exam question but you may be provided with extracts.

Sections 3.9 to 3.13 (pages 31-43)

The rest of this section focuses on the key concepts of consumer surplus and producer surplus. Read through carefully, understanding how consumer surplus, producer surplus and total surplus all relate. Example 10 on page 34 and the graph on page 35 are useful to overview. In section 3.13 be able to picture the impact of a price ceiling; a price floor; a tax on buyers and a tax on sellers on surpluses. The graphs on pages 37-41 demonstrate these concepts well and being able to understand the dynamics will help in the exam. Generally, you will not be provided with any graphical illustrations in the exam but the graph will be described in words so being able to recall and reproduce the graph may quickly help you to determine the answer to the question.

Section 4 Demand Elasticities (pages 43-53)

An important section to finish with, so read through carefully. At first the equations look daunting but if you are struggling, make use of the last two points in the summary section at the end of the reading on page 55. Exhibit 22 on page 49 provides a good pictorial representation of how elasticity and total expenditure relate. It's important that you work through all three parts of example 13 on page 53.

Question practice

- Attempt all 26 questions at the back of the reading, starting on page 56. Again, the solutions beginning on page 60 provide useful explanations for the correct answer.

2 hours

- In addition, all questions in the BPP Question Bank should be attempted prior to the exam.

STUDY SESSION 4 – READING 14

Demand and Supply Analysis: Consumer Demand (page 63)   **4 hours**

Importance level   **Medium**

Key areas

- Consumer theory
- Indifference curves, opportunity sets and how budget constraints impact on consumer decisions
- The effects of substitution and income on demand
- Normal good, an inferior good, a Giffen good and a Veblen good

Content review – CFA curriculum

The focus of this reading is the origination of the demand curve.

Section 2 Consumer Theory (page 64)

This section introduces consumer choice theory. This is the theory that takes consumer preferences and budget constraints and develops the consumer demand curve. Read through as an introduction to the rest of the reading.

Section 3 Utility Theory (pages 64-74)

This section tackles the first part of consumer theory which is modelling consumer preferences and tastes. Make use of exhibits 1 to 5 (pages 68-73) as you delve into utility functions and indifference curves, as these will help understand the narrative. Both examples 2 (page 70) and 3 (page 74) help put the theory into real life examples.

Section 4 The Opportunity Set: Consumption, Production and Investment Choice (pages 74-79)

This section tackles the second part of consumer choice theory and that is budget constraint. The learning outcome statement in this area does ask you to 'calculate' the budget constraint so make sure you work through example 4 on page 77 in its entirety. The investment opportunity set detailed in Section 4.3 only needs a quick read through as this is covered in detail later in the portfolio management section of your studies.

3 hours

Section 5 Consumer Equilibrium (pages 79-82)

This section brings together consumer preferences and budget constraints and develops the demand curve. Make sure you are happy with what each point represents in exhibit 11 on page 80. Be able to understand the impact of a change in income on both a normal and inferior good. Understand how the change in price impacts on the demand curve in both an elastic and inelastic example.

Section 6 Revisiting the Consumer's Demand Function (pages 82-90)

This section rounds off the reading by examining substitution and income effects for different types of goods. Work through all of this section but pay particular attention to understanding Giffen goods (section 6.4, page 88) and Veblen goods (section 6.5, page 90) as these are specifically mentioned in the learning outcome statement.

The summary beginning on page 90 is a useful revision guide.

BPP
LEARNING MEDIA

Question practice

- Attempt all 8 questions at the back of this reading on page 92.

- In addition, all questions in the BPP Question Bank should be attempted prior to the exam.

1 hour

STUDY SESSION 4 – READING 15

Demand and Supply Analysis: The Firm (page 95)

5 hours

Importance level   **High**

Key areas

- Total, average and marginal revenue

- Total, average, marginal, fixed and variable costs

- Breakeven points of production in the short and long run

- Impact of economies of scale on average total costs in short and long run

- Total, marginal, and average product of labour

- Diminishing marginal returns

Content review – CFA curriculum

In contrast to the previous reading which looked into the demand curve, this reading delves into the make-up of the supply curve and the associated 'theory of the firm'. This reading looks at profit maximisation for firms in a perfect competition environment. Later on in Reading 16, you will be introduced to other types of market structures such as monopolies.

Section 2 Objectives of the Firm (pages 96-101)

The main objective of the firm is to maximise profit. This section sets out the definition of profit and is relatively straight forward, needing a quick read through and focusing on the definitions in bold. Exhibit 2 at the end of the section provides a good summary of terms and relationships.

Section 3 Analysis of Revenue, Costs and Profits (pages 102-133)

This is a key part of the reading and it is essential that you get to grips with all the terms and calculations in exhibit 3 on page 102. This will help you later when trying to interpret cost and revenue graphs for the firm.

In Section 3.1.1 on page 103, you must understand what is meant by total revenue, average revenue and marginal revenue. Make good use of exhibits 5 (page 105) and 6 (page 106) which summarise the inter-relationships under both perfect competition and imperfect competition.

3 hours

In Section 3.1.3 on page 109, you must understand what is meant by total cost, total fixed cost, total variable cost, the marginal costs and average costs. Exhibit 12 (page 111) is crucial to understand and shows the inter-relationship between the marginal and average costs.

Now that you understand the key relationships, the rest of section 3 builds on this. Make sure you are happy with where the breakeven and shutdown point is for a firm, as shown in exhibit 17 (page 116). Example 5 on page 118 is good to work through as a summary of the key points.

Make sure you are happy with the idea of profit maximisation in Section 3.1.4 on page 120 and work through all parts of example 7 (page 123). Exhibit 26 (page 124) provides a much needed summary of profit maximisation, as well as loss minimisation strategies for firms. This concept is revisited in Section 3.1.6 on page 129 when profit maximisation in the long run is explored.

Section 3.1.5 on page 125 brings in economies and diseconomies of scale and the effect on average total costs. Exhibit 27 (page 126) gives a good pictorial summary of the impact on long-run average total costs. Section 3.1.7 on page 132 on long run industry supply curves is straight forward and needs a quick read through.

Section 3.2 Productivity (pages 134-142)

This last part of the reading looks at labour as an input to production and how output per worker is calculated and used. Make good use of exhibit 35 (page 135) which defines the key terms and calculations. Understanding the idea of diminishing marginal returns is key in section 3.2.2 on page 136 and it is important that you work through example 10 on page 137. Make sure you are happy with the descriptions of all the areas depicted in exhibit 39 (page 139) and recognize that the productivity graph mirrors the cost graph you have seen before in section 3.1.3.

Finally, work through the last few pages of the reading, attempting both example 11 (page 140) and 12 (page 141) to cement the idea that firms aim to maximise output per monetary unit of input cost.

As always, the summary on pages 142-3 is a very useful revision guide.

Question practice

- Attempt questions 1 to 25 at the back of the reading on pages 144-148.

- In addition, all questions in the BPP Question Bank should be attempted prior to the exam.

2 hours

Key areas

- Perfect competition
- Monopolistic competition
- Oligopoly
- Pure monopoly

Content review – CFA curriculum

Section 2 Analysis of Market Structures (pages 152-156)

This section introduces the four distinct market structures: perfect competition; monopolistic competition; oligopoly; and pure monopoly. This introduction should be relatively straightforward and as long as you are happy to be able to regenerate the contents of exhibit 1 (page 155), this is sufficient coverage.

As the learning outcome statements for this reading ask you to compare each of the market structures, as you go through, for each market structure, jot down the following in your own summary table:

- What is the relationship between price, MR, MC, and economic profit (draw a graph)?
- What is the elasticity of demand?
- What is the shape of the supply function?
- What is the profit maximising price and output quantity?
- What factors affect the long-run equilibrium?
- What is the pricing strategy?

Section 3 Perfect Competition (pages 156-171)

2 hours

You should already be familiar with most of the characteristics of perfect competition as much of the previous reading on Demand and Supply Analysis of the Firm, focused on this market structure. Elasticity of demand in section 3.1.1 (page 158) and consumer surplus in section 3.1.3 (page 162) are repeats of the points made in Reading 13, Basic Principles and Concepts. The rest of this section just needs a read through to refresh the shape of the cost/quantity graphs and the relationships between marginal revenue and marginal costs covered in the previous reading.

Section 4 Monopolistic Competition (pages 171-175)

The key element of a monopolistic competition market is product differentiation. All companies make economic profits in the short run but they will not in the long run.

Section 5 Oligopoly (pages 175-184)

Make sure you understand that strategic behaviour is a key element of an oligopoly and then be able to describe the three basic pricing strategies: pricing interdependence; the Cournot assumption, and the Nash equilibrium. Be able to summarise the optimal price and output for an oligopoly and recognise that in the long run oligopolies can make economic profits.

Section 6 Monopoly (pages 185-193)

One of the key points to understand is the price setting strategies and how a monopoly might come to its pricing decision as illustrated in exhibit 19 (page 190). Example 4 on page 193 is a good test of whether you understand monopolies compared to perfect competition. This is the style of economics questions that you may face, so it is not all about the detail in the graphs that you need to remember but the bigger picture and key points.

Section 7 Identification of Market Structure (pages 193-196)

This section needs a quick read through and a basic understanding of a concentration ratio and calculating a HHI (Herfindahl-Hirschman Index). The HHI is frequently tested. Example 5 on page 196 however is about as hard as it gets, provided you can recall the calculation this should pose no issues in the exam.

The summary on page 196 is an essential revision guide.

Question practice

- Complete all 19 questions at the back of the reading on pages 198-201.

- In addition, all questions in the BPP Question Bank should be attempted prior to the exam.

2 hours

NOTES

STUDY GUIDANCE

Economics: Macroeconomic Analysis

This guidance aims to identify the topics that we consider to be of premium importance for your exam preparation.

Study session 5 (Volume 2) comprises of:

Reading 17   Aggregate Output, Prices, and Economic Growth

Reading 18   Understanding Business Cycles

Reading 19   Monetary and Fiscal Policy

Recommended study time is 12 hours of work.

 Exam focus

Economics represents 10% of the exam. This session is likely to represent approximately 3 - 4% of the exam. There is a lot of material for a relatively small percentage of the exam and it is important therefore to focus on the key points which are more likely to be examined. You are not expected to be an economist and the examination only tests your understanding of a few core areas within economics.

 Pre-requisites

Complete study session 4 before attempting this study session.

STUDY SESSION 5 – READING 17

Aggregate Output, Prices, and Economic Growth (page 207)   **4 hours**

Key areas

- GDP, national income, personal income and personal disposable income

- Relationship between savings, investment, fiscal balance and trade balance

- IS and LM curves and combining to give the aggregate demand curve

- Shifts in the aggregate demand and supply curves

- Sustainability of economic growth

Content review – CFA curriculum

Section 2 Aggregate Output and Income (pages 208-226)

This section looks at the first step in macroeconomic analysis which is measuring the size of an economy. This can be achieved by measuring GDP. Know the three broad criteria used in measuring GDP and work through exhibit 2 (page 212) to understand that a value-of-final-output approach and a sum-of-value-added approach to measurement, yield the same result. Exhibit 4 (page 214) on the underground economy makes for interesting reading but is not covered by a learning outcome statement so can be ignored. Know the relationship between nominal and real GDP and learn the formula for the GDP deflator on page 215. Example 2 (page 216) should be worked through.

Exhibit 6 (page 218) is an excellent mind map when understanding the components of GDP. Sections 2.2.2 and 2.2.3 need only a quick read through and are low priority.

Section 2.3 (page 221) on the calculation of GDP and other income measures should be worked through slowly and use example 3 on page 224 to test your knowledge.

Section 3 Aggregate Demand, Aggregate Supply and Equilibrium (pages 226-263)

This is a key section which you should go through carefully. Equation 2 (page 227) is an important one to remember as it gives the drivers of private saving. Also important is the quantity theory of money equation in section 3.1.2 (page 234). You will revisit the quantity theory of money later on in Reading 19, Monetary and Fiscal Policy. Make sure you understand what the IS and IM curves represent and appreciate that they combine to give the aggregate demand curve.

2 hours

In section 3.3 (page 240), the three questions in the first paragraph set the scene for the next two sections. These are very detailed sections but are important. Make use of exhibit 18 (page 246) which summarises shifts in the aggregate demand curve and example 8 on page 246 should be worked through. Exhibit 20 (page 251) provides a good summary of the factors shifting aggregate supply and example 11 (page 251) is a good test of your knowledge. Monetary and fiscal policy need only a brief read through as these are covered in detail later in Reading 19, Monetary and Fiscal policy.

Understand the four types of macroeconomic equilibrium in section 3.4 (page 253) (long-run full employment; short-run recessionary gap; short-run inflationary gap; short-run stagflation).

Section 3.4.5 (page 260) is an excellent end to this part of the reading, summarising the impact of shifts in AD and AS in isolation and together.

Section 4 Economic Growth and Sustainability (pages 263-276)

Be able to distinguish between the uses of growth in real GDP and per capita GDP. Know the two-factor production function equation in section 4.1 and understand how growth in technology, labor and capital combine to give growth in potential GDP. The most important example to work through is example 17 (page 273) at the end of the reading.

The summary on pages 276-279 is a useful revision guide for this reading.

Question practice

- You should attempt all 35 questions at the back of this reading as all are exam style questions (pages 280-284).

2 hours

- In addition, all questions in the BPP Question Bank should be attempted prior to the exam.

STUDY SESSION 5 – READING 18

Understanding Business Cycles (page 289)   **4 hours**

Importance level   **Medium**

Key areas

- Phases of the business cycle
- Types and measures of unemployment
- Inflation, disinflation, and deflation
- Economic indicators

Content review – CFA curriculum

Section 2 Overview of the Business Cycle (pages 290-304)

Read through this section focusing on the different phases of the business cycle and using exhibit 1 (page 292) as a good summary. Work through examples 1 to 6 as you read through, as they are all exam style questions.

Section 3 Theories of the Business Cycle (pages 305-313)

This section needs a quick read through, understanding the key elements of Neoclassical, Keynesian, Monetarist, and New Classical schools of thought.

Section 4 Unemployment and Inflation (pages 313-328)

An important section to get to grips with as these are two topics regularly examined. Know the various definitions used in the labor markets and work through example 10 (page 316). Read through the different types of inflation; don't get bogged down in the calculations of inflation, focus on the indices used and any limitations. Examples 13, 14 and 16 are all good tests of multiple choice questions in this area.   **2 hours**

Section 5 Economic Indicators (pages 328-335)

There is a lot of detail in this section but you need to focus on two things: firstly knowing the uses and limitations of the different economic indicators and that leading indicators tend to be the most useful; and secondly, being presented with economic indicators and being able to identify the business cycle phase this implies. Read through exhibit 7 (pages 330-331) and the rest of the section but then test yourself with the questions in example 19 (page 334) and those at the back of the reading.

The summary on page 336 is a useful revision guide.

Question practice

- There are 25 questions at the back of this reading starting on page 338 – you should attempt them all.   **2 hours**
- In addition, all questions in the BPP Question Bank should be attempted prior to the exam.

Key areas

- Definition of money
- Fisher effect
- Role of the central banks
- Monetary policy and its limitations
- The tools of fiscal policy
- Arguments for being concerned by a fiscal deficit
- Interaction of monetary and fiscal policy

Content review – CFA curriculum

This section picks up on the detail of monetary and fiscal policy that was briefly introduced in Reading 17, Aggregate Output, Prices and Economic Growth, when talking about shifts in the aggregate supply curve.

Section 2 Monetary Policy (pages 348-386)

Understand the definition and function of money. Use exhibit 2 (page 351) to understand the creation process of money. Familiarise yourself with the quantity theory of money in section 2.1.4 (page 354) which you saw earlier in Reading 17. The Fisher effect in section 2.1.7 (page 358) is an important theory to understand. Example 5 (page 360) on the UK Thatcher era of inflation and example 6 (page 361) on the Northern Rock bank run make for good reading but are low priority. The rest of this section is lengthy and needs a brief read through only.

2 hours

Section 3 Fiscal Policy (pages 386-404)

This section needs a read through, and given the current world economy, an area you would be well advised to read is arguments for and against being concerned about national debt, just before exhibit 14 (page 388). Know the fiscal tools listed in section 3.2 (page 394).

Section 4 The Relationship between Monetary and Fiscal Policy (pages 404-408)

This section needs a read through and attempt all three questions in example 19 (page 407).

Question practice

- There are 33 questions at the back of this reading beginning on page 410 – you should attempt them all.

- In addition, all questions in the BPP Question Bank should be attempted prior to the exam.

2 hours

BPP
LEARNING MEDIA

NOTES

STUDY GUIDANCE

Economics: Economics in a Global Context

This guidance aims to identify the topics that we consider to be of premium importance for your exam preparation.

Study session 6 (Volume 2) comprises of:

Reading 20   International Trade and Capital Flows

Reading 21   Currency Exchange Rates

Recommended study time is 8 hours of work. Please add additional 2 hours to complete Progress Test 3.

 Exam focus

Economics represents 10% of the exam. This session is likely to represent approximately 3 - 4% of the exam. There is a lot of material for a relatively small percentage of the exam and it is important therefore to focus on the key points which are more likely to be examined. You are not expected to be an economist and the examination only tests your understanding of a few core areas within economics.

 Pre-requisites

Complete study sessions 4 and 5 before attempting this Study Session.

Key areas

- GDP and GNP

- Benefits and costs of international trade

- Types of trade restrictions and agreements

- Balance of payments

Content review – CFA curriculum

Section 2 International Trade (pages 420-439)

Read through this section quickly as an introduction. It introduces the key terms so make sure you focus on the bolded words. There was a new LOS introduced for the 2013 sitting that compares GDP with GNP so make sure you have understood this at the beginning of Section 2.1. Section 2.3 (page 427) is an important section on the benefits and costs of international trade. Flick to the summary at the back of the reading for a good overview (page 472). Work through all of section 2.4 (page 431) as you need to be able to distinguish between comparative advantage and absolute advantage. Example 3 on page 432 is essential to work through and understand. This section also introduces two traditional models of comparative advantage, Ricardian and Heckscher-Ohlin models. You need to appreciate their distinguishing features: the Ricardian model focuses on technology differences between countries, whereas the Heckscher-Ohlin model concentrates on factor endowments (capital and labor) differences between countries.

Section 3 Restrictions and Agreements (pages 440-453)

Read through each of the different types of trade restrictions: tariffs, quotas, export subsidies and trading blocs, understanding what they are and the impact they have on trade. Example 6 on page 444 provides a good test of this knowledge. Recognize that capital restrictions, detailed in section 3.5 (page 450), limit the trading on financial markets rather than goods market as trade restrictions do.

2 hours

Section 4 Balance of Payments (pages 453-465)

This is a section that you need an overview only. Make sure you know the components of the balance of payments and what they include: current account, capital account, and financial account. Section 4.3 can be skipped through as it is low priority. Section 4.4 (page 461) needs a careful read through as it expands the GDP (Y) equation that you saw back in Reading 17 into a definition of the current account (equation 3 on page 461). The current account can also be expressed in terms of private sector savings (Sp) and government savings (Sg) in equation 10 (page 462). Knowing these two equations will help you understand what makes the current account move and hence the balance of payments. Example 11 on page 463 is a good one to work through to understand the dynamics.

Section 5 Trade Organisations (pages 466-472)

Needs a quick read through so that you can identify the functions and objectives of each of the international organisations: World Bank, IMF, World Trade Organisation.

The summary on page 472 is a very useful revision guide for this reading.

Question practice

- There are 24 questions at the back of this reading starting on page 476 all of which are in exam format. It is worth attempting all of them.

- In addition, all questions in the BPP Question Bank should be attempted prior to the exam.

2 hours

Key areas

- Real and nominal exchange rates

- Spot rates and forward rates

- Forward calculations

- Exchange rate regimes

- How the exchange rate impacts on the balance of payments

Content review – CFA curriculum

This reading introduces the foreign exchange market by looking at basic terminology for exchange rates and some of the economics associated with exchange rate movements.

Section 2 The Foreign Exchange Market (pages 485-502)

This section introduces the basic concepts of foreign exchange quotes. Know the relationship between the nominal exchange rate (those quoted) and the real exchange rate (adjusted for ratio of price levels). Sections 2.1 (page 490) and 2.2 (page 496) are lengthy but from it make sure you understand how a forward rate compares to a spot rate, and the functions and key participants of the FX market. Example 2 on page 494 is a comprehensive example that will test your understanding of forward rates.

Section 3 Currency Exchange Rate Calculations (pages 502-516)

It is important that you can deal with both a direct and indirect quote for currencies as you could be presented with either. No need to worry about exhibit 6 as you will not be tested on this. Know how to calculate the appreciation or depreciation of a currency as a percentage. There is a worked example of this in the narrative at the end of section 3.1 (page 504) and example 5 (page 507) will test this as well as testing section 3.2 on cross rate calculations.

2 hours

Section 3.3 (page 509) needs to be worked through on forward calculations. Afterwards you need to be able to answer all five parts of example 6 (page 514).

Section 4 Exchange Rate Regimes (pages 516-527)

This section needs a quick read through and if you can answer the six parts of example 7 on page 525, your coverage is sufficient.

Section 5 Exchange Rates, International Trade and Capital Flows (page 516)

This section ties exchange rates back to macroeconomic concepts that you saw in Study Session 5. A trade deficit (surplus) is matched by a capital account surplus (deficit). Read through the two approaches to how exchange rates impact the trade balance: the elasticities approach (section 5.1, page 529) and the absorption approach (section 5.2, page 533). Example 8 on page 534 provides very good practice of exam style questions in this area.

The summary starting on page 537 is a useful revision guide.

Question practice

- There are 21 questions at the back of this reading starting on page 541 and you should attempt them all.

- In addition, all questions in the BPP question bank should be attempted prior to the exam.

2 hours

CHECKPOINT – END OF STUDY SESSIONS 4, 5 AND 6

You are now able to attempt the **Progress Test 3 on Economics.**

2 hours

BPP
LEARNING MEDIA

Progress Test 3 – Economics

Questions

1. Which of the following statements is *least appropriate* regarding cross-price elasticities of demand?

   A. The cross-price elasticity of substitute products is positive.

   B. Goods with negative cross-price elasticity of demand are called normal goods.

   C. The smaller the magnitude of the cross-price elasticity, the weaker the relationship between the two goods.

2. The market demand function for household gas usage is given by the equation:

   $Q_g = 96 - 2.4P_g + 0.9I + 0.8P_o$

   Where Q_g is the average number of gas units consumed in one year, P_g is the average price per gas unit, I is the average household annual income in thousands of pounds, and Po is the average price of domestic heating oil.

   Assume that P_g is equal to 24, I is equal to 50, and P_o is equal to 9.

   The price elasticity of demand for gas is *closest* to:

   A. −2.4

   B. −0.6

   C. +0.8

3. When demand for a good is price inelastic, then an increase in units sold will cause total revenue to:

   A. Rise and marginal revenue to be negative.

   B. Fall and marginal revenue to be positive.

   C. Fall and marginal revenue to be negative.

4. Market A is characterized by the following:

   - Few sellers

   - Homogenous product

   - High barriers to entry

   - Some pricing power of the firm

   - High degree of advertising spend

   Market A is *best* described as a(n):

   A. Monopoly.

   B. Oligopoly.

   C. Monopolistic competition.

5. Which of the following is *most* likely to be an argument in favour of being concerned about the size of a national debt?

    A. Higher levels of debt may lead to higher tax rates.

    B. A proportion of the money borrowed may have been used for capital investment projects.

    C. The 'Ricardian equivalence' may mean that the private sector increase their savings.

---

6. At a price of $80, good X has a unitary price elasticity of demand. Which of the following is *most accurate* given a rise in price to $85?

    A. The revenue will increase.

    B. The revenue will decrease.

    C. The revenue will remain unchanged.

---

7. The following graph relates to a monopoly.

    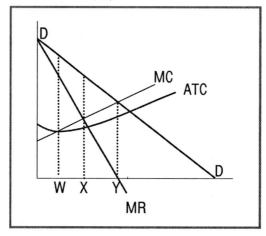

    At what quantity would the firm produce in equilibrium?

    A. Point W.

    B. Point X.

    C. Point Y.

---

8. Which of the following statements about the conditions necessary to achieve the specified outcomes is correct?

    A. Firms wishing to maximize their profits should increase output until marginal revenue exceeds marginal costs.

    B. Firms wishing to minimize costs should produce such that marginal costs equal average costs.

    C. Competitive firms aiming to maximize sales revenue should set price equal to marginal cost.

---

9. Which of the following are Central Banks *least* likely to use in controlling money supply?

    A. Changing reserve requirements.

    B. Open market operations.

    C. Verbal communication with banks.

10. In a perfectly competitive market where marginal cost intersects average total cost at a point below marginal revenue for an individual firm:

   A. Companies are making economic (supernormal) profits.

   B. The market is in permanent disequilibrium.

   C. Companies will shut down production, temporarily or permanently.

11. In the context of money supply, which of the following *best* describes money neutrality?

   A. In the long run, an increase in the money supply leads to an increase in prices and unemployment and output are unaffected.

   B. In the long run, an increase in the money supply leads to an increase in output and prices are unaffected.

   C. In the long run, an increase in the money supply leads to a decrease in unemployment, an increase in output and no change in prices.

12. If a profit-maximizing firm finds that its marginal revenue exceeds its marginal cost, the firm should:

   A. Increase output no matter whether the firm is a price taker or a price setter.

   B. Decrease output no matter whether the firm is a price taker or a price setter.

   C. Increase output if the firm is a price taker but not necessarily if the firm is a price setter.

13. Which of the following is *least* likely to be subtracted from national income to calculate personal income?

   A. Indirect business taxes.

   B. Corporate income taxes.

   C. Unemployment benefit.

14. The primary burden of a tax will fall most heavily on buyers when:

   A. The demand curve is flatter than the supply curve.

   B. The supply curve is flatter than the demand curve.

   C. The demand and supply have equal steepness.

15. When a price floor is imposed above the market equilibrium level:

   A. A shortage will result.

   B. A surplus will result.

   C. There will be no impact on the market.

16. Which of the following statements is *least accurate*?

   A. The short run marginal cost curve cuts both the short run average variable cost curve and the short run average total cost curve at their minimum points.

   B. The long run average total cost curve is the envelope of all the short run possibilities.

   C. There is one plant size that can produce at all points on the long run average total cost curve.

17.   In macroeconomics, the crowding-out effect refers to:

    A. The impact of government deficit spending on inflation.

    B. A situation in which the unemployment rate is below its natural rate.

    C. The impact of government borrowing on interest rates and private investment.

18.   Which of the following statements regarding a straight-line demand curve with a flat (horizontal) slope is *most accurate*?

    A. It will exhibit price inelasticity only.

    B. It will exhibit price elasticity only.

    C. It will exhibit price elasticity and price inelasticity only.

19.   Calculate the economic profit of a firm with the following information:

	$
Revenue	300,000
Salaries paid	100,000
Rental income foregone	30,000
Accounting depreciation	10,000
Economic depreciation	20,000
Normal profit	50,000

    A. $90,000

    B. $100,000

    C. $110,000

20.   Which of the following is a *limitation* of the concentration ratio for identifying market structure?

    A. It does not quantify market power.

    B. It is impacted upon by mergers between the top market incumbents.

    C. It is impacted by the elasticity of demand.

21.   Which of the following is *least likely* to be an automatic stabilizer?

    A. Progressive income taxes.

    B. Unemployment compensation benefits.

    C. Import tariffs.

22.   The reserve requirement is 10% and the Fed sells $20m of Treasury bonds. What will be the *most likely* impact of this on money supply?

    A. Increase by $200m.

    B. Decrease by $200m.

    C. Increase by $2m.

23. Which of the following is *most likely* to cause the velocity of money to increase, other things being equal?

    A. Real output falling.

    B. Prices rising.

    C. Money supply rising.

24. Which of the following statements *most closely* describes a private value auction?

    A. Each buyer places a subjective value on an item and the values are likely to differ.

    B. Each buyer bids for an item that has the same value to all bidders.

    C. Bids are elicited from potential buyers and buyers cannot see the other bids until the auction is over.

25. Which of the following *most closely* describes the impact of both a decrease in Aggregate Demand and a decrease in Aggregate Supply?

	AGGREGATE PRICE LEVEL	REAL GDP
A.	Indeterminate	Increase
B.	Indeterminate	Decrease
C.	Decrease	Indeterminate

26. Which of the following biases of a Laspeyres inflation index can be overcome by calculating the Fisher Index?

    A. Substitution bias.

    B. Quality bias.

    C. New product bias.

27. Which of the following is *most likely* to increase aggregate demand, all else being equal?

    A. An increase in taxes.

    B. An increase in Government spending.

    C. A decrease in bank reserves.

28. Which of the following statements best describes monopolistic competition?

    A. A large number of sellers with low barriers to entry.

    B. A small number of sellers with high barriers to entry.

    C. A large number of sellers with complete freedom of entry and exit.

29. Which one of the following statements *most accurately* states the difference between accounting profit and economic profit?

    A. Accounting profit understates economic profit as it includes all expenses including such items as depreciation, amortization and interest expense.

    B. Accounting profit understates economic profit, as it includes explicit and implicit costs whereas economic profit considers only explicit cost.

    C. Accounting profit overstates economic profit, as no allowance is made for the implicit cost of equity capital.

30. Which of the following statements is the primary determinant of price elasticity of demand?

    A. Consumer choice and income.

    B. Whether complementary goods can be found.

    C. Whether substitutes for the good are available.

Progress Test 3 – Economics

Answers

1.   **B**   A normal good is one with a positive own-price elasticity of demand. A negative cross-elasticity of demand means the goods are complements

See LOS 13m

2.   **B**   From the demand function $\Delta Q_g/\Delta P_g = -2.4$ (coefficient of own price)

Solve for Q_g:

$Q_g = 96 - (2.4 \times 24) + (0.9 \times 50) + (0.8 \times 9)$

$\quad = 90.6$

At $P_g = 24$, $\Delta Q_g/\Delta P_g \times P_g/Q_g$

$\quad = -2.4 \times 24/90.6$

$\quad = -0.6$

See LOS 13m

3.   **C**   Inelastic demand means that we are at the right side of the demand curve. As a result, marginal revenue is negative and total revenue must be falling

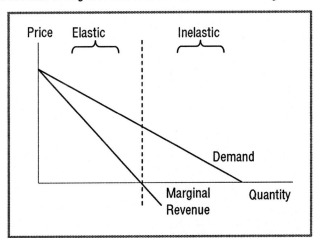

Alternatively think of 'inelastic' as 'unresponsive', so, the price drops but the increase in quantity is proportionally less. Therefore, the drop in price does not cause an overall increase in revenue

See LOS 15b

4.   **B**   In an oligopoly, a small number of firms dominate the market

See LOS 16a

5.   **A**   Both B and C are arguments against being concerned about national debt. In B, capital investment may lead to increased productivity in the future, and in C private sector may save in anticipation of increased taxes and offset the impact of the deficit

See LOS 19m

6. **B** Price elasticity of demand = –1 at $80, therefore any price movement will lead to a decrease in a firm's revenue. If P rises, we move onto the elastic part of the demand in which case the quantity demanded will fall by a greater percentage than the percentage increase in price. Conversely, if P falls, we move onto the inelastic part of the demand area, in which case the quantity demanded will rise but by a smaller percentage than the fall in P

   See LOS 13m

7. **B** MR = MC for a profit-maximizer

   See LOS 16d

8. **B** The marginal cost curve cuts the average total cost curve at its minimum value

   See LOS 16b

9. **C** The three primary tools are open market operations; the refinancing rate; and reserve requirements

   See LOS 19f

10. **A** The firm will produce at the point where MC = MR

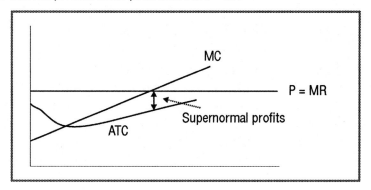

   See LOS 15g

11. **A** Money neutrality is the phenomenon whereby an increase in the money supply leads to an increase in prices in the long run and has no affect on real variables such as output and labour

   See LOS 19c

12. **A** This is the profit maximization rule applicable to both price takers and price setters

   See LOS 16d

13. **C** Unemployment benefit is added to national income to derive personal income as it is a type of transfer payment that is not earned but received from the government

   See LOS 17d

14. **B** The relative burden from a tax falls disproportionately on the group that has the steeper curve

See LOS 13j

15. **B** When a price floor is imposed sellers would like to sell more at he higher price (above the equilibrium) but buyers would choose to buy less at the higher price. The consequence is that a result a surplus results

See LOS 13k

16. **C** There is no one plant size that can produce at all points on the long run average total cost curve

See LOS 15h

17. **C** Government spending financed by borrowing will drive up interest rates reducing the amount of borrowing possible by the private sector. As a result, private investment will fail

See LOS 19n

18. **B** A flat demand curve allows infinite quantity of a good to be sold at the market price. If the price rises, consumers buy nothing. For example, a single seller in a perfectly competitive market could face a horizontal demand curve: farmer selling wheat can sell all at the market price, but if he raises the prices he will sell none as consumers will go elsewhere for the exact same product. Therefore a horizontal demand curve has infinite elasticity and is called perfectly elastic. It exhibits only price elasticity

See LOS 13m

19. **B** $300,000 - 100,000 - 30,000 - 20,000 - 50,000 = \$100,000$

Accounting depreciation is excluded as it is neither an explicit cost (costs paid in money) or an implicit cost (a foregone alternative action). Economic depreciation is the implicit cost of using capital and is the change in market value over a given period

See LOS 15a

20. **A** The concentration ratio takes *no* account of the elasticity of demand, and is *not* impacted by mergers of the larger players. The fact that the concentration ratio is *not* impacted by demand elasticity and mergers are in themselves limitations of the concentration ratio. The correctly stated limitation is that the concentration ratio does not quantify market power

See LOS 16f

21. **C** Import transfers do not automatically vary with the economic cycle

See LOS 19l

22. **B** $\$20m \times \dfrac{1}{0.1}$ will be taken out of the money supply

See LOS 19b

23. **B** MV = PY. If P increases (inflation) then more transactions would be required from a constant money supply

See LOS 19c

24. **A** B is the definition of a common value auction and C describes a sealed bid auction

See LOS 13h

25. **B** A decrease in both AD and AS means real GDP and unemployment will decline but the impact on price level is not clear unless we know the size of the decreases

See LOS 17i

26. **A** The Fisher Index is the geometric mean of the Laspeyres Index and the Paasche Index. The Laspeyres Index keeps the composition of the basket in the *base year* constant, whereas the Paasche Index keeps the *current* composition of the basket constant. When prices moves the substitution effect means that consumers tend to switch to the cheaper products, as a result the Laspeyres Index tends to *overstate* inflation and the Paasche Index will tend to *understate* inflation. By taking the geometric mean of both indices, the substitution bias is mitigated

See LOS 18g

27. **B** All the other options would result in a decrease in aggregate demand

See LOS 17h

28. **A** Monopolistic competition describes a large number of sellers supplying differentiated products to a market with low barriers to entry. Sellers of a differentiated product, but with high barriers to entry describes an oligopoly. A purely competitive market (also known as a price-taker market) has a large number of sellers with complete freedom of entry and exit

See LOS 16a

29. **C** While accounting profit and economic profit are both calculated by subtracting costs from revenues, the definition of total cost differs. Economic total cost includes implicit costs, whereas accounting total cost excludes the implicit cost of equity capital. An implicit cost is the opportunity cost for use of resources owned by the company

See LOS 15a

30. **C** Price elasticity of demand is determined by the availability of substitutes. When substitutes for a product can be purchased, price increases cause consumers to switch to other products. If substitutes cannot be found, demand for the product will be inelastic

See LOS 13m

STUDY GUIDANCE

Financial Reporting and Analysis (FRA): An Introduction

This guidance aims to identify the topics that we consider to be of premium importance for your exam preparation.

Study session 7 (Volume 3) comprises of:

Reading 22   Financial Statement Analysis: An Introduction

Reading 23   Financial Reporting Mechanics

Reading 24   Financial Reporting Standards

Recommended study time is 8.5 hours of work.

 Exam focus

Overall Financial Reporting and Analysis (study sessions 7, 8, 9, and 10) represents 20% of the exam and is the largest individual subject matter of the exam. There will be 24 questions in each of the morning and afternoon papers. Therefore you must plan your study time accordingly, especially if accounting is a new area for you make sure you.

You are not expected to be an accountant but you are expected to be able to analyse accounts.

The exam will test your understanding of how accounts work which as in other areas will test your conceptual understanding rather than ability to construct accounts.

You are expected to understand key accounting ratios and most importantly be able to interpret what the ratios might mean.

You will also be tested on the impact of different accounting policies and your ability to compare accounts prepared in slightly different ways.

One thing to note is that the Financial Reporting is partly based on American rules and procedures so even if you are an accountant or familiar with accounting it is important that you understand the CFA requirements.

There are a lot of areas of repetition with a number of important concepts introduced in the early readings which are then the subject of complete readings later on (e.g. inventory valuation).

Throughout the text there are a lot of detailed examples, most from real companies and their accounts. It is not necessary to go through these examples in most instances, the exam questions will be simple and more conceptual and you are not expected to plough your way through large or complex accounts.

 Pre-requisites

There are no pre-requisites for the study session.

STUDY SESSION 7 – READING 22

Financial Statement Analysis: An Introduction (page 5)

3 hours

Importance level

High

Key areas

- What are the key financial statements and supplementary information
- Objectives of financial reporting including the role of auditors
- Financial statement analysis framework

Content review – CFA curriculum

If you are an accountant or extremely familiar with accounts you can probably skip sections 1-3, and go straight to the summary at the end of the chapter as a reminder. You should however read section 4 (see below for necessary reading).

Section 2 Scope of Financial Statement Analysis (pages 6-11)

Understand the role of financial reporting and who might use the information.

Look at example 1 on page 7 to understand the difference between profit and cash flow. This is a key concept of which your understanding will be examined.

You do not have to go through exhibits 1 and 2.

Section 3 Major Financial Statements and Other Information Sources (pages 11-31)

Although we go into much more detail in later readings including how to interpret the various accounting statements and how they interact, it is key that you understand what is meant by

- Income statement
- Balance sheet
- Cash flow statement
- Financial notes and supplementary schedules
- Role of auditors and what is meant by the auditor's report

2 hours

If you feel clear immediately as to what these statements are and their roles then you will be able to read through the text quite quickly.

It is worth looking briefly at the Volkswagen exhibits on page 13 but it is not necessary to go through them in detail.

Section 4 Financial Statement Analysis Framework (pages 31-35)

Section 4.1 (page 32) and exhibit 11 (page 32) cover everything you need to know on this area.

The summary beginning on page 36 is a useful revision guide.

Question practice

- Attempt all the 8 questions at the end of this reading on page 38.
- In addition, all questions in the BPP Question Bank should be attempted prior to the exam.

1 hour

Financial Reporting Mechanics (page 41)   **4 hours**

Key areas

- Interaction of accounting statements
- Accruals concept

This reading acts as an introduction for later readings and a lot of the concepts are covered in more detail later on.

Content review – CFA curriculum

If you are an accountant or extremely familiar with accounts you still need to look at this section to understand the CFA/American interpretation of accounts and the accounting equations.

Section 2 Classification of Business Activities (pages 42-43)

It is important to understand this at this stage although it is covered more later on.

Section 3 Accounts and Financial Statements (pages 43-45)

Read the introduction and skip to exhibit 2 (page 45). Look at the section regarding current and non-current assets.

Section 3.2 Accounting Equations (pages 46-51)

Read this section carefully focusing on the numbered equations 1a – 5b (pages 46-48).

It is worth going through this section, paying particular attention to the interaction of the basic statements and key items in the financial statements.

You need work through exhibits 3 and 4 and it is worth testing yourself by attempting examples 2 (page 50) and 3 (page 51).

2 hours

Section 4 The Accounting Process (pages 51-69)

This section is non-key and does not need to be read. All necessary concepts are covered elsewhere.

Section 5 Accruals and Valuation Adjustments (pages 69-72)

It is key to understand the accruals concept covered in section 5.1 although it will be gone into in more detail elsewhere.

Section 6 Accounting Systems (pages 72-73)

Although not a key section do look at the debit and credit section 6.2.

Section 7 Using Financial Statements in Security Analysis (pages 73-75)

It is worth reading this section quickly and look at the Worldcom example number 4 (page 74).

The summary on page 75 is a short revision guide.

Appendix 23

If you are struggling with the concept of accounts and accounting then Appendix 23 on page 77 may be useful.

Question practice

- It is worth attempting all 20 of the practice questions starting on page 95, they are realistic questions and the type of which will come up in the exam.

- Make sure that you understand the answers referring back to the text where necessary.

2 hours

- In addition, all questions in the BPP Question Bank should be attempted prior to the exam.

STUDY SESSION 7 – READING 24

Financial Reporting Standards (page 101)   **1.5 hours**

Key areas

- This reading is of relatively low priority although there are some sections that need to be learnt for the exam

Content review – CFA curriculum

It is suggested that unless you have time you only read in detail

- Section 5.2 (pages 120-121) Qualitative Characteristics of Financial Statements

- Summary (pages 140-141)

30 minutes

Question practice

- Attempt all 18 of the practice problems at the back of this reading starting on page 142.

- In addition, all questions in the BPP Question Bank should be attempted prior to the exam.

1 hour

NOTES

STUDY GUIDANCE

FRA: Income Statements, Balance Sheets, and Cash Flow Statements

This guidance aims to identify the topics that we consider to be of premium importance for your exam preparation.

Study session 8 (Volume 3) comprises of:

Reading 25   Understanding Income Statements

Reading 26   Understanding Balance Sheets

Reading 27   Understanding Cash Flow Statements

Reading 28   Financial Analysis Techniques

Recommended study time is 18 hours of work.

 Exam focus

Overall Financial Reporting and Analysis (study sessions 7, 8, 9 and 10) represents 20 % of the exam and is the largest individual subject matter of the exam. There will be 24 questions in each of the morning and afternoon papers. Therefore you must plan your study time accordingly especially if accounting is a new area for you make sure you.

You are not expected to be an accountant but you are expected to be able to analyse accounts.

The exam will test your understanding of how accounts work which as in other areas will test your conceptual understanding rather than ability to construct accounts.

You are expected to understand key accounting ratios and most importantly be able to interpret what the ratios might mean.

You will also be tested on the impact of different accounting policies and your ability to compare accounts prepared in slightly different ways.

One thing to note is that the Financial Reporting is partly based off American rules and procedures so even if you are an accountant or familiar with accounting it is important that you understand the CFA requirements.

There are a lot of areas of repetition with a number of important concepts introduced in the early readings which are then the subject of complete readings later on (e.g. inventory valuation).

Throughout the text there are a lot of detailed examples, most from real companies and their accounts. It is not necessary to go through these examples in most instances, the exam questions will be simple and more conceptual and you are not expected to plough your way through large or complex accounts.

 Pre-requisites

There are no pre-requisites for this study session.

Key areas

- Components and format of the income statement
- Revenue recognition – principles
- Expense recognition – principles
- Non-recurring items
- Earnings per share

Content review – CFA curriculum

Section 2 Components and Format of the Income Statement (pages 151-155)

Review this section and look at exhibit 1 (page 151) in order to understand how simple income statements are presented.

Also review exhibit 3 (page 155) and understand what is meant by gross profit and net income.

Section 3 Revenue Recognition (pages 155-168)

Understand the general principles of revenue recognition and the two main methods of income recognition in long-term contracts.

Work through examples 2 (page 162) and 3 (page 163).

Sections 3.2 and 3.3 are not key and can just be read through quickly.

Section 4 Expense Recognition (pages 169-173)

Understand the general principles and specifically understand what is meant by cost of goods sold. Read through example 8 (page 171) which is comprehensive.

Inventory valuation is covered in detail later in Reading 29 so can be skipped over briefly at this stage.

2 hours

Section 4.2 Issues in Expense Recognition (pages 173-178)

This section can be read through quite quickly as depreciation is covered in detail in Reading 30. Do make sure though you understand what is meant by depreciation and the nature of the calculations. This is required to understand some of the issues in cash flow preparation in Reading 27.

Section 5 Non-Recurring Items (pages 178-184)

You need to understand the different accounting treatments, implications and different income / expense presentation of items that are not likely to reoccur.

Section 6 Earnings Per Share (pages 185-194)

This section is an introduction to this topic, which is quite frequently examined. You should work through the examples (examples 12-19) showing how to deal with stock splits and share issues. You may prefer to leave this section until you are more familiar with accounts.

Section 7 Analysis of the Income Statement (pages 194-198)

Understand what is meant by common size analysis – exhibit 15 is a good summary.

Section 8 Comprehensive Income (pages 198-201)

Read through this section because it provides a very good summary. Attempt example 21 on page 200.

Read through the summary on page 201 as a revision guide.

Question practice

- Attempt all 20 practice problems at the back of the reading on page 204.

- In addition, all questions in the BPP Question Bank should be attempted prior to the exam.

2 hours

Key areas

- Format and components of the balance sheet

- Measurement bases of assets and liabilities

- Common-size balance sheets

Content review – CFA curriculum

Section 2 Components and Format of the Balance Sheet (pages 212-217)

You need to understand what is meant by assets and liabilities and the different types.

It is also crucial you understand what is meant by equity.

Section 2.2 Current and Non-current Classification (pages 215-216)

Learn the distinctions between current and non-current items.

Sections 3-5 Current Assets, Current Liabilities, Non-current Assets, and Non-current Liabilities (pages 217-241)

You need to learn the key ways in which assets and liabilities are classified and measured (e.g. historic cost, fair value). After this you need only read through the rest of section 3 and 4 quite briefly as the important points are covered in more detail in later readings. Exhibit 8 (page 228) is a good example of the balance sheet. Other exhibits do not need to be gone through.

2 hours

Section 6 Equity (pages 242-246)

You need to understand the components of equity and what factors can cause it to change in value.

Section 7 Analysis of the Balance Sheet (page 246)

There is a new learning outcome statement on common-size balance sheets so work through section 7.1 and practice with example 6 (page 249).

Read the summary starting on page 256 as it is a useful revision guide.

Question practice

- Attempt questions 1 to 23 beginning on page 259.

- In addition, all questions in the BPP Question Bank should be attempted prior to the exam.

2 hours

Key areas

- Classification of cash flows
- Direct and indirect cash flow formats
- Preparation of a cash flow statement
- Cash flow statement analysis

Content review – CFA curriculum

Section 2 Components and Format of the Cash Flow Statement

Section 2.1 Classification (pages 267-269)

This section is key; it is worth reading this section thoroughly working through examples 1 (page 268) and 2 (page 269).

Section 2.2 A Summary of Differences Between IFRS and U.S GAAP (pages 269-270)

You will need to learn this, it is frequently examined. Look at exhibit 1 on page 270 and put it to memory.

Section 2.3 Direct and Indirect Methods (pages 270-280)

It is worth looking at the BPP slides for this section to compare the two methodologies then looking at the definition in the CFA book.

You need not go through the exhibits 2-5 and can then jump to section 3.

Section 3 The Cash Flow Statement: Linkages and Preparation (pages 280-295)

You need to be able to prepare a basic cash flow statement, deriving numbers from balance sheets and income statements.

2 hours

This entire section is worth reading to look at specific calculations involved in deriving the cash flows. Examples 3-7 in the text represent likely sorts of exam questions and should be worked through.

Section 4 Cash Flow Statement Analysis (page 295)

The two key parts of this section are

- Evaluation of the sources and uses of cash
- Free cash flow to the firm and free cash flow to equity
- Cash flow ratios

Look at the four steps involved in evaluation on page 295. It is not necessary to work through the examples or the exhibits in section 4.1.

Make sure you understand section 4.3 (page 303) on free cash flows and the importance of this concept. Go through exhibit 15 on page 305 in detail to understand the performance ratios, their calculations and what it measures. Work through example 10 (page 305) then look at the solution.

Read the summary starting on page 306 as it is a useful revision guide.

Question practice

- All 23 questions at the back of this reading starting on page 308 should be attempted. You may wish to do half now and the other half closer to the exam to help with revision. They are all in exam format and represent likely sorts of exam questions.

- In addition, all questions in the BPP Question Bank should be attempted prior to the exam.

2 hours

Key areas

- Ratio analysis

- DuPont equation

This section is key as it is a fundamental part of an investment analyst's job. It is important to understand why you calculate certain ratios and what they mean as well as how to do the calculations themselves. You are more likely to be asked which ratio you would use or be able to interpret the results of a ratio calculation as to just performing a simple calculation.

Content review – CFA curriculum

Section 2 The Financial Analysis Process (pages 318-322)

Section 2.1 Objectives and section 2.2 Computations and Analysis.

These sections are introductory and can be read through quickly; it is not necessary to work through the examples.

Section 3 Analysis Tools and Techniques (pages 322-338)

This section describes why analysts may want to use ratios and how. You can read through this section quite quickly, most of it is of low importance, common sense or you will be able to understand through other readings. The most important section is 3.1.2 (page 328) Value, Purposes and Limitations of Ratio Analysis. This is the most likely area on which you will be examined.

Section 4 Common Ratios Used in Financial Analysis (page 338)

It is key to understand exhibit 9 on page 339 and the different categories of financial ratios and what they are broadly used for.

Section 4.1 Interpretation and Context (pages 339-340)

Read through quickly.

4 hours

Section 4.2 Activity Ratios (pages 340-342)

Exhibit 10 (page 340) lists all the activity ratios you need to know. Note that the denominator is always based on the average. This means it will be the average of the balance sheet number at the beginning of the period and end of the period.

Exam Tip

A number of students forget to use the average balance sheet number and will just use the closing balance sheet. In the exam you will likely be given extracts from the two balance sheets or the average number.

Read the text and work through example 6 on page 342.

Section 4.2.2 Interpretation of Activity Ratios (pages 342-346)

It is worth going through this section carefully. It explains the ratios listed in exhibit 10 and how to interpret them. You need to understand which ratios you want to see high numbers and which ratios you want to see low numbers. As well as reading the text work through examples 7 (page 343) and 8 (page 345).

Section 4.3 Liquidity Ratios (pages 346-351)

This section follows the same format as the activity ratios.

You should look at exhibit 12 on page 347 then work through carefully the interpretation of the ratios. Also work through example 9 (page 349).

Section 4.4 Solvency Ratios (pages 351-355)

This section follows the same format as the activity ratios.

You should look at exhibit 14 on page 353 then work through carefully the interpretation of the ratios. Also work through example 11 (page 354).

Section 4.5 Profitability Ratios (pages 355-359)

This section follows the same format as the activity ratios.

You should look at exhibit 15 on page 356 then work through carefully the interpretation of the ratios. Also work through example 12 (page 358).

Section 4.6 Integrated Financial Ratios (pages 359-361)

If you have understood the previous sections then section 4.6.1 is of low priority.

Section 4.6.2 DuPont Analysis: The Decomposition of ROE (pages 362-366)

It is key you learn equations 1a (page 362) and 1b (page 363). It is also crucial you understand what the equations mean and how analysts use it. Equation 1c (page 364) is less key but useful to know if you can.

Work through example 15 on page 364. Example 16 is lower priority.

Section 5 Equity Analysis (page 367)

This section follows the same format as the activity ratios etc focusing on valuation ratios.

It is a key section to understand.

You should look at exhibit 18 on pages 368-370 then work through carefully the interpretation of:

- Earnings per share
- Dividend payout ratios (although this comes up later in the equities section)

Sections 5.2 and 5.3 are low priority (pages 370-373)

Sections 6, 7 and 8 are low priority (pages 373-379)

The summary on page 380 is quite concise for this chapter focusing on a few key concepts.

Question practice

- We recommend that you attempt questions 1 to 22 at the back of this reading, starting on page 382.

- In addition, all questions in the BPP Question Bank should be attempted prior to the exam.

2 hours

STUDY GUIDANCE

FRA: Inventories, Long-lived Assets, Income Taxes, and Non-current Liabilities

This guidance aims to identify the topics that we consider to be of premium importance for your exam preparation.

Study session 9 (Volume 3) comprises of:

Reading 29   Inventories

Reading 30   Long-lived Assets

Reading 31   Income Taxes

Reading 32   Non-current (Long-term) Liabilities

Recommended study time is 16 hours of work.

 Exam focus

Overall Financial Reporting and Analysis (study sessions 7, 8, 9, and 10) represents 20% of the exam and is the largest individual subject matter of the exam. There will be 24 questions in each of the morning and afternoon papers. Therefore you must plan your study time accordingly especially if accounting is a new area for you make sure you.

You are not expected to be an accountant but you are expected to be able to analyse accounts.

The exam will test your understanding of how accounts work which as in other areas will test your conceptual understanding rather than ability to construct accounts.

You are expected to understand key accounting ratios and most importantly be able to interpret what the ratios might mean.

You will also be tested on the impact of different accounting policies and your ability to compare accounts prepared in slightly different ways.

One thing to note is that the Financial Reporting is partly based off American rules and procedures so even if you are an accountant or familiar with accounting it is important that you understand the CFA requirements.

There are a lot of areas of repetition with a number of important concepts introduced in the early readings which are then the subject of complete readings later on (e.g. inventory valuation).

Throughout the text there are a lot of detailed examples, most from real companies and their accounts. It is not necessary to go through these examples in most instances, the exam questions will be simple and more conceptual and you are not expected to plough your way through large or complex accounts.

 Pre-requisites

You should complete study sessions 7 and 8 before attempting this study session.

STUDY SESSION 9 – READING 29

Inventories (page 393)

4 hours

Importance level

Very high

Key areas

- Inventory valuation methods and comparison
- Calculation of cost of sales

Content review – CFA curriculum

Section 2 Cost of Inventories (page 395)

This section can be read through quickly.

Section 3 Inventory Valuation Methods (page 396)

Make sure you understand the four calculation methods (sections 3.1-3.4) on page 397.

Section 3.5 Calculation of Cost of Sales (page 398)

Work through Example 2 on page 398, attempting all the solutions.

Section 3.6 Periodic v Perpetual Inventory Systems (page 400)

Low priority and does not need to be studied.

Section 3.7 Comparison of Inventory Methods (page 402)

2 hours

Read this section so you understand the implications of the different methodologies, although the emphasis on this has now moved to CFA level II.

Section 4 Measurement of Inventory Value (page 402)

Low priority and the important points are covered in the summary.

Section 5 Presentation and Disclosure (page 404)

Low priority and the important points are covered in the summary.

Section 6 Evaluation of Inventory Management (page 405)

Low priority and the important points are covered in the summary.

Read the summary on page 412 especially if you have missed out sections 4-6.

Question practice

- All 25 questions in at the back of this reading starting on page 414 should be attempted as most are in exam format. They probably cover the whole spectrum of potential exam questions and will re-enforce your reading.

2 hours

- In addition, all questions in the BPP Question Bank should be attempted prior to the exam.

Long-lived Assets (page 425)   **4 hours**

Importance level   **Very high**

Key areas

- Depreciation methods
- Intangible assets

Content review – CFA curriculum

Section 2 Acquisition of Long-lived Assets (page 426)

Read through this section as an introduction.

Section 2.1 Property, Plant and Equipment (pages 428-430)

Understand example 1 on page 428, capitalising versus expensing and example 2 on page 430, effect of capitalised borrowing costs.

Section 2.2 Intangible Assets (pages 431-435)

You need to read this section understanding what is meant by intangible assets, how they are created, accounting rules and the impact on the accounts.

Section 3 Depreciation and Amortisation of Long-lived Assets (pages 435-445)

The key is to understand the different depreciation methodologies and the impact that different methodologies have on the accounts at different stages. Example 4 on page 436 is a comprehensive example of the different methodologies.

You do not need to look at example 5 in detail or section 3.2 on amortisation.

Section 4 The Revaluation Model (pages 445-448)

This section is lower priority and can be read through quickly.   **2 hours**

Section 5 Impairment of Assets (pages 448-450)

This section is lower priority and can be read through quickly. You should pick up on the difference between the US approach of first setting an impairment test (using undiscounted cash flows) and the IFRS approach where there is no need to do a test first.

Section 6 Derecognition (pages 451-453)

This section is of higher importance and you need to be able to calculate the impact on the accounting statements of the sale or disposal of a long-lived asset.

Section 7 Presentation and Disclosures (page 453-459)

This section can be read through quickly. It is not necessary to go through the examples.

Section 8 Investment Property (pages 460-462)

This section was added to last year's reading so make sure that you understand how the accounting for an investment property differs from the accounting for property, plant, and equipment.

Read the summary starting on page 462 for revision purposes before attempting the practice questions.

Question practice

- Attempt questions 1 to 22 starting on page 465 as these are a good indication of exam standard questions.

2 hours

- In addition, all questions in the BPP Question Bank should be attempted prior to the exam.

A lot of students struggle with some of concepts and calculations especially relating to deferred tax. Focus on the core basic concepts and you will still be able to answer most possible questions.

Key areas

- Differences between accounting and taxable income
- Concept of deferred tax

Content review – CFA curriculum

Section 2 Differences Between Accounting Profit and Taxable Income (pages 474-479)

Read through this section completely including example 1 on page 477. This is the most key area in understanding how you might be examined on taxation.

Section 3 Determining the Tax Base of Assets and Liabilities (pages 480-485)

In this section the key thing is to understand the concepts rather than the detailed calculations especially the calculations involved in changing tax rates.

Section 4 Temporary and Permanent Differences between Taxable and Accounting Profit (pages 485-489)

You must understand what the implications are for permanent differences as opposed to temporary (sections 4-4.2) and look at exhibit 1 on page 487 for a summary of the treatment of temporary differences.

You do not need to work through example 4 and the remainder of section 4 is not key either.

2 hours

Section 5 Unused Tax Losses and Tax Credits (pages 489-490)

Read through this section in order to understand the accounting rules relating to this.

Section 6 Recognition and Measurement of Current and Deferred Tax (pages 490-494)

This section is lower priority.

Section 7 Presentation and Disclosures (pages 494-500)

This section can be read through quickly. It is not necessary to go through the examples.

Section 8 Comparison of IFRS and US GAAP (pages 500-502)

Low priority, this section can be ignored.

Read the summary on page 503 for revision purposes, it covers all the key concepts before attempting the practice questions.

Question practice

- Attempt all 22 questions at the back of this reading starting on page 504. It is unlikely that there would be more than 1 or 2 questions like this in the exams and if you understand the concepts well you might intuitively be able to deduce the answer.

- For questions where you are struggling focus on the solution given and the reasons why the answer is correct.

2 hours

- In addition, all questions in the BPP Question Bank should be attempted prior to the exam.

Key areas

- Debt finance (bonds payable)
- Leases
- Pensions

The key is to learn the accounting rules for debt finance and leases rather than just understanding what the products are. Pensions is very much an overview at this level.

Content review – CFA curriculum

Section 2 Bonds Payable (pages 512-529)

Sections 2.1 and 2.2 (pages 512-520) are the most key and should be gone through thoroughly including examples 1-4. If you are reading this section before you have done the fixed income section you may want to consider looking at Reading 53 first as an introduction to bonds.

Sections 2.3-2.6 are lower priority and the examples 5-9 are not necessary to go through.

Section 3 Leases (pages 529-547)

Sections 3.1 and 3.2 are key sections. The examples are long and overly detailed. You do not need to work through all the examples but must cover the following:

- Leasing v Buying (section 3.1) – page 530
- Types of lease – finance or operating (section 3.2) – pages 530-531

It is key to understand the rules which allow a lease to be classified as finance lease.

2 hours

- Accounting for leases by the lessee (section 3.2.1) – page 531
- Accounting for leases by the lessor (section 3.2.2) – page 542

Exhibit 2 on pages 546-7 is a very useful summary of the financial statement impact of leases and if you learn this you will have covered the section comprehensively.

Section 4 Introduction to Pensions and Other Post-employment Benefits (pages 547-550)

This is low priority and the summary section covers the important points. Pensions are a topic covered in detail at Level II.

Section 5 Evaluating Solvency: Leverage and Coverage Ratios (pages 550-554)

This section is an extension of previously covered ratios. Look at exhibit 3 (page 551) as this covers all the ratios.

Read the summary starting on page 554 for revision purposes and to cover pensions.

Question practice

- All 16 practice questions should be attempted starting on page 556. Make sure you understand the answers referring to the text where necessary.

2 hours

- In addition, all questions in the BPP Question Bank should be attempted prior to the exam.

NOTES

STUDY GUIDANCE

FRA: Evaluating Financial Reporting Quality and Other Applications

This guidance aims to identify the topics that we consider to be of premium importance for your exam preparation.

Study session 10 (Volume 3) comprises of:

Reading 33   Financial Reporting Quality: Red Flags and Accounting Warning Signs

Reading 34   Accounting Shenanigans on the Cash Flow Statement

Reading 35   Financial Statement Analysis: Applications

Recommended study time is 4 hours of work. An additional 2 hours should be added to complete Progress Test 4.

 ## Exam focus

Overall Financial Reporting and Analysis (study sessions 7, 8, 9 and 10) represents 20% of the exam and is the largest individual subject matter of the exam. There will be 24 questions in each of the morning and afternoon papers. Therefore you must plan your study time accordingly especially if accounting is a new area for you make sure you.

You are not expected to be an accountant but you are expected to be able to analyse accounts.

The exam will test your understanding of how accounts work which as in other areas will test your conceptual understanding rather than ability to construct accounts.

You are expected to understand key accounting ratios and most importantly be able to interpret what the ratios might mean.

You will also be tested on the impact of different accounting policies and your ability to compare accounts prepared in slightly different ways.

One thing to note is that the Financial Reporting is partly based on American rules and procedures so even if you are an accountant or familiar with accounting it is important that you understand the CFA requirements.

There are a lot of areas of repetition with a number of important concepts introduced in the early readings which are then the subject of complete readings later on (e.g. inventory valuation).

Throughout the text there are a lot of detailed examples, most from real companies and their accounts. It is not necessary to go through these examples in most instances, the exam questions will be simple and more conceptual and you are not expected to plough your way through large or complex accounts.

 ## Pre-requisites

You must work through the previous study sessions on FRA before attempting this one.

STUDY SESSION 10 – READING 33

Financial Reporting Quality: Red Flags and Accounting Warning Signs (page 563p)

1 hour

Importance level   Low

Key areas

- Accounting warning signs
- Low quality of earnings

Content review – CFA curriculum

Read briefly through sections 2 and 3 and focus on being able to answer the four learning outcome statements. Section 4 (page 572) on Enron and section 5 (page 577) on Sunbeam are interesting reading but you do not need to go through them for the exam.

30 minutes

Question practice

- Attempt all 11 practice problems at the back of this reading starting on page 581.
- In addition, all questions in the BPP Question Bank should be attempted prior to the exam.

30 minutes

STUDY SESSION 10 – READING 34

Accounting Shenanigans on the Cash Flow Statement (page 585)   **1 hour**

Importance level   Low

Key areas

- Manipulating the cash flow statement

Content review – CFA curriculum

This reading is short and needs a quick read through. Be able to quote the four ways of manipulating the cash flow statement. Do not worry about the exact mechanics of the share buyback issue.   **30 minutes**

Question practice

- Attempt all 10 questions at the back of this reading starting on page 593.

- In addition, all questions in the BPP Question Bank should be attempted prior to the exam.   **30 minutes**

STUDY SESSION 10 – READING 35

Financial Statement Analysis: Applications (pages 597)   **2 hours**

Key areas

- There are no key areas in this reading. If you have a good understanding of the financial reporting and analysis readings up to now, most aspects of this reading will be very straight forward. This reading is just an application of what you have already learnt

Content review – CFA curriculum

Read the introduction section to understand what is meant by financial statement analysis. After this, read through the rest of the reading quickly and revise with the summary at the end, starting on page 639.   **1 hour**

Question practice   **1 hour**

- Attempt all 14 practice problems at the back of this reading starting on page 642.

- In addition, all questions in the BPP Question Bank should be attempted prior to the exam.

CHECKPOINT – END OF STUDY SESSIONS 7, 8, 9 AND 10

You are now able to attempt the **Progress Test 4 on Financial Reporting and Analysis**.   **2 hours**

NOTES

Progress Test 4 – Financial Reporting and Analysis

Questions

The following information relates to Questions 1, 2 and 3. Assume US GAAP applies.

	$
Dividend payments	2,000
Payments to suppliers	50,000
Issue of common stock	60,000
Interest payments	4,000
Receipts from customers	170,000
Wages	30,000
Machinery purchased	40,000
Retirement of debt	20,000
Machinery sold	1,000

1. Cash flows from investing activities are:

   A. ($35,000).

   B. ($39,000).

   C. ($40,000).

2. Cash flows from operating activities are:

   A. $84,000.

   B. $86,000.

   C. $90,000.

3. Cash flows from financing activities are:

   A. $34,000.

   B. $36,000.

   C. $38,000.

4. Which of the following statements regarding the classification of dividends paid is *most accurate*?

   A. Under US GAAP, dividends paid are always a financing cash flow whereas under IAS GAAP they may also be an investing cash flow.

   B. Under US GAAP, dividends paid are always a financing cash flow whereas under IAS GAAP they may also be an operating cash flow.

   C. Under US GAAP, dividends paid are always an operating cash flow whereas under IAS GAAP they may also be an investing cash flow.

5. A company has a tax rate of 35% and incurred interest cost of $200,000. EBIT was $1,500,000 from sales of $10,000,000 and a total asset base of $4,000,000.

    The return on equity has been established as 30%. What was the financial leverage multiplier?

    A. 0.26.

    B. 1.42.

    C. 2.50.

6. Which of the following is *least likely* to be a step in the financial statements analysis framework?

    A. Interpret processed data.

    B. Feedback to management.

    C. Articulate the purpose and context of analysis.

7. Which of the following is *least* likely to be true of a valuation allowance?

    A. A valuation allowance arises when it is probable that deferred tax assets will not be recovered.

    B. A reversal of a valuation allowance can occur.

    C. An analyst will ignore the valuation allowance when assessing a company's overall deferred tax position.

8. Total sales are $80,000. Total assets are $60,000 and total liabilities are $10,000. The net profit margin is 10%. The return on equity (ROE) is *closest to*:

    A. 6%.

    B. 10%.

    C. 16%.

9. A company has inventory turnover of 10, payables turnover of 20 and receivables turnover of 15. The company's cash conversion cycle is *closest to*:

    A. 25.0 days.

    B. 30.5 days.

    C. 42.5 days.

10. Taco Inc purchases an asset with a two-year life and no expected scrap value for $10,000. The asset is to be written down to zero using straight-line depreciation.

    Taco Inc attracts tax allowances in respect of this asset of $8,000 in the first year and $2,000 in the second year. Tax rates are 40% in the first year and 35% in the second year.

    Based on the above, the deferred tax asset or liability on the balance sheet will show:

	YEAR END 1	YEAR END 2
A.	$1,200 liability	$1,050 asset
B.	$1,200 liability	$0
C.	$1,050 liability	$0

11. If a lessee firm treats a lease as an operating lease instead of capitalizing it, the effect on the following will be:

	CURRENT RATIO	DEBT/EQUITY RATIO
A.	Increase	Decrease
B.	Decrease	Increase
C.	No change	Decrease

12. Comparison of firms with capital leases versus those with operating leases would show the companies with capital leases reporting:

    A. Higher operating cash flows.

    B. Lower operating cash flows.

    C. Higher current ratios.

13. Capitalization of interest in *most likely* to be:

    A. Permitted under US GAAP and permitted under International Financial Reporting Standards.

    B. Permitted under US GAAP but not permitted under International Financial Reporting Standards.

    C. Not permitted under US GAAP but permitted under International Reporting Standards.

14. Which of the following statements concerning accounting inventories is *least accurate*?

    A. LIFO means more recently acquired items are treated as sold first.

    B. FIFO and LIFO methods are used for inventories of items that are not interchangeable.

    C. US GAAP does not permit a company to reverse a previous writedown of inventory values.

15. BondIssuer Inc. issues 5% coupon bonds with a $1,000,000 par value for $1,044,500. The bonds are redeemable at par in five years' time. The market interest rate at the time of issue is 4%. Which of the following statements is *most accurate* in respect of BondIssuer Inc.'s accounting for the debt in the year of issue?

    A. The interest charged to the income statement will be more than that charged in cash flow from operations by $8,220.

    B. The interest charged to the income statement will be the same as that charged in cash flow from operations.

    C. The balance sheet liability at the end of the first year will be $1,036,280.

16. A company has sales of $5,000 and a net profit margin of 13%. Its tax retention ratio is 65% and its interest coverage is 2.67×. The pre-interest profit margin is *closest to*:

    A. 32%.

    B. 29%.

    C. 22%.

17. Which of the following inventory valuation method will give the highest gross profit in times of declining prices?

    A. LIFO.

    B. FIFO.

    C. Weighted average cost.

18. If an analyst wishes to make an adjustment to treat operating leases as capital leases, the *most appropriate* adjustment would be to increase the company's:

    A. Return on assets.

    B. Debt to equity ratio.

    C. Interest coverage.

19. Which one of the following would *most likely* to be a warning sign that income could be overstated?

    A. Expensing operating costs.

    B. Capitalising current year expenditures and amortising over future years.

    C. Shifting operating expenses related to future period to the current period.

20. In a stable price environment with replacement of long-lived assets but no growth, which of the following statements regarding a company which uses accelerated depreciation of assets as opposed to straight-line depreciation is *most accurate*?

    A. Accelerated depreciation policies will result in lower total asset turnover, but will not affect operating profit margins.

    B. Accelerated depreciation policies will result in lower operating profit margins, but will have no impact on total asset turnover.

    C. Accelerated depreciation policies will result in higher total asset turnover but will not affect operating profit margins.

21. Which of the following statements is *most accurate*?

    A. A higher residual value will give a higher depreciation charge under straight-line depreciation.

    B. Straight-line depreciation gives a rising return on capital.

    C. Changing the estimated useful life of an asset is a change in accounting principle.

22. An analyst details the following information about a company:

Estimated operating profit for the year	$165m
Estimated interest payable for the year	$25m
Effective tax rate for the year	30%
Retained earnings at the beginning of the year	$1,560m
Estimated dividends for the year	$80m

Which of the following is *closest to* the retained earnings at the end of the year?

A. $1,578m.

B. $1,620m.

C. $1,658m.

23. Disposal and discontinuance of a division of a company is treated as:

A. A separate item net of taxes in the income statement.

B. A change in accounting principle.

C. An extraordinary item.

24. Which of the following is *least likely* to be characteristic of an effective reporting framework?

A. Enhances transparency of a company's financial statements.

B. Valuation of assets and liabilities reflect far values.

C. Ensures reasonable consistency across companies and time periods.

25. Which of the following would *most likely* cause a weighted average calculation in the simple earnings per share calculation?

A. Repurchase of stock during the year.

B. A stock dividend during the year.

C. Issue of convertible debt partway through the year.

26. Given the transactions listed below, and assuming US GAAP applies, cash flows from operating activities (CFO) using the direct method is *closest to*:

	$
Interest expense	(50)
Dividends paid	(20)
Retirement of stock	(45)
Cash payments to suppliers	(200)
Sale of machinery	50
Purchase of vacant land	(10)
Cash payment for salaries	(135)
Cash collections	500
Purchase of machinery	(100)

A. $95.

B. $115.

C. $145.

27. A company conducts an impairment review and discovers it needs to write-down the value of a large number of assets. Which of the following statements regarding the impact on total asset turnover and on the profit margin in the year of the impairment review is *most accurate*?

	TOTAL ASSET TURNOVER	PROFIT MARGIN
A.	Increase	Increase
B.	Decrease	Decrease
C.	Increase	Decrease

28. The *most likely* impact of the securitisation of receivables on the following is:

	RECEIVABLES TURNOVER	OPERATING CASH FLOW
A.	Increase	Increase
B.	Increase	Decrease
C.	Decrease	Increase

29. Which of the following statements *most accurately* describes a complex capital structure?

A. Outstanding securities include common stock and nonconvertible preferred stock.

B. Outstanding securities include common stock, nonconvertible bonds, and nonconvertible preferred stock.

C. Outstanding securities include common stock, convertible bonds, and nonconvertible preferred stock.

30. A company has net income of $100,000, depreciation of $10,000 and interest of $20,000. In addition, they have a lease with a present value of $40,000 and an estimated lease interest expense of $5,000. The company's cash flow coverage of financial fixed costs is *closest to*:

A. 4.6×

B. 5.0×

C. 5.4×

Progress Test 4 – Financial Reporting and Analysis

Answers

1. **B**

Capital expenditure	(40,000)
Proceeds from sale of machinery	1,000
	(39,000)

    See LOS 27a

2. **B**

Customers	170,000
Suppliers	(50,000)
Wages	(30,000)
Interest paid	(4,000)
	86,000

    See LOS 27a

3. **C**

Dividend payments	(2,000)
Stock issue	60,000
Retired debt	(20,000)
	38,000

    See LOS 27a

4. **B**   Dividends received are an operating cash flow under US GAAP but under IAS GAAP may also be an investing cash flow

    See LOS 27c

5. **B**   Using the extended Dupont system

    $$ROE = (1 - tax) \times \frac{EBT}{EBIT} \times \frac{EBIT}{Sales} \times \frac{Sales}{Total\ Assets} \times Leverage$$

    $$30\% = (1 - 0.35) \times \frac{1,300}{1,500} \times \frac{1,500}{10,000} \times \frac{10,000}{4,000} \times Leverage$$

    $30\% = 21.125\% \times Leverage$

    $1.42 = Leverage$

    See LOS 28d

6. **B**   The last step is 'follow-up' by updating reports and recommendations. Feedback to management is not part of the process

    See LOS 22f

7. **C** An analyst will not ignore a valuation allowance, instead will scrutinise any changes in the valuation allowance

    See LOS 31g

8. **C** Net income = 10% × $80,000 = $8,000

    Stockholders' equity = $60,000 − $10,000 = $50,000

    $$\text{ROE} = \frac{8,000}{50,000} = 16\%$$

    See LOS 28d

9. **C** Average number of days in inventory = 365/10 = 36.5

    Average receivables collection period = 365/15 = 24.33

    Average payables payment period = 365/20 = 18.25

    Cash conversion cycle = 36.5 + 24.33 − 18.25 = 42.5 days

    See LOS 28e

10. **C** The deferred tax liability or asset should reflect the tax rate expected to apply when the deferred tax reverses (i.e. in Year 2)

	Year 1 $	Year 2 $
Depreciation	5,000	5,000
Tax allowance	(8,000)	(2,000)
Timing difference	(3,000)	3,000
Recognized at next year's tax rate (35%)	(1,050)	(1,050)
	Deferred tax charge	Deferred tax credit
Closing balance sheet	Deferred tax liability (1,050)	Deferred tax liability –

    See LOS 31d

11. **A** A capital lease will show a long-lived asset and a liability. Some of the liability will be short-term (in current liabilities) and the rest will be long-term (in noncurrent liabilities). An operating lease will show nothing on the balance sheet at all

    See LOS 32g

12. **A** With an operating lease all the payments are treated as an operating expense and as such are deducted from cash flow from operators

    See LOS 32g

13. **A** Capitalization of interest is permitted under both sets of standards

    See LOS 30a

14. **B**   If inventories of items are not interchangeable then the 'specific identification' method can be used. FIFO and LIFO are used when inventory items *are* interchangeable

       See LOS 29b

15. **C**   The carrying amount of the liability at issue is $1,044,500. The interest payment on the cash flow statement will be the physical cash interest paid of 5% on the face value, i.e. $50,000. The interest that goes through the income statement will be the effective interest expense (4% × $1,044,500) of $41,780. The balance sheet value of the liability at the beginning of year one will be the initial carrying value, $1,044,500 plus effective interest of $41,780, less actual interest paid of $50,000, giving $1,036,280

       See LOS 32b

16. **A**   Note that this is not an easy question. Always be aware of how long you are taking to answer such questions and don't be afraid to move on if you feel you are getting bogged down

	$
Sales	5,000
Costs ($5,000 – $1,599)	(3,401)
EBIT	1,599
Interest (*see below*)	(599)
EBT ($650 ÷ 0.65)	1,000
Income tax ($1,000 – $650)	(350)
Net income ($5,000 × 0.13)	650

Interest cover = 2.67 = EBIT ÷ Interest

EBT + Interest = EBIT

2.67 = (EBT + Interest) ÷ Interest = (EBT ÷ Interest) + 1

1.67 = EBT ÷ Interest

Interest = EBT ÷ 1.67 = $1,000 ÷ 1.67 = $599

$$\frac{EBIT}{Sales} = \frac{\$1599}{\$5000} = 32\%$$

       See LOS 28c

17. **A**   When prices are declining, LIFO will mean the most recently purchased (cheaper) stock will be expensed through cost of sales. So cost of sales will be low and gross profit will be high

       See LOS 29e

18. **B**   Return on assets and interest coverage would both fall

       See LOS 35e

19. **B**   Expensing operating costs is appropriate. Shifting operating expenses from future periods to current periods will *understate* profits. Capitalising and amortising will result in shifting current expenses to future periods (e.g. Worldcom example) and hence *overstate* profits

       See LOS 33d

20. **C**

	Accelerated	Straight Line
NBV of Assets	Lower	Higher
Total Assets	Lower	Higher
Equity	Lower	Higher
Sales	Same	Same
Depreciation charges	Same	Same
Operating profit	Same	Same

With accelerated depreciation

$$\text{Total asset income} = \frac{\text{Sales}}{\text{Total assets}} = \frac{\text{Same}}{\text{Lower}} \therefore \text{Higher}$$

$$\text{Operating profit margin} = \frac{\text{Operating profit}}{\text{Sales}} = \frac{\text{Same}}{\text{Same}} \therefore \text{Same}$$

See LOS 30c

21. **B** The higher the residual value, the lower the annual depreciation charge. Changing the estimated useful life of an estimate is a change in accounting estimate

See LOS 30c

22. **A** Net income for the year = $(165 - 25) \times 0.7 = 98$

End of year retained earnings = $1,560 + 98 - 80$

= $1,578$

See LOS 23e

23. **A** These are shown after income from continuing operations but before extraordinary items (if using US GAAP, remember no extraordinary items allowed under IFRS)

See LOS 25e

24. **B** How assets and liabilities are valued is a barrier to a coherent reporting system, not a characteristic (transparency, comprehensiveness, consistency). Valuations can be based on fair values, historic cost and current cost)

See LOS 24g

25. **A** Note that the issue of convertible debt may cause a weighted average calculation for a fully diluted calculation

See LOS 25g

26. **B**   Cash collections are an operating cash inflow, as are salaries, payments to suppliers, and interest expense

Cash flow from operations therefore equals

$500 – $50 – $200 – $135 = $115

The purchase and sale of machinery and the purchase of land are all investing cash flows. The retirement of common stock and payment of dividends are both financing cash flows

See LOS 27f

27. **C**   The impairment review will cause assets to fall and so total asset turnover will increase. The profit margin will fall in the year of the impairment as the reduction in the value of the assets is taken through the income statement

See LOS 30h

28. **A**   Accounts receivables fall and cash is received

See LOS 34

29. **C**   A complex capital structure includes convertible debt or equity securities, which, if exercised, would require the issuance of common stock. The issuance of new common stock would dilute or lower earnings per share (EPS)

See LOS 25g

30. **C**   Cash flow coverage of financial fixed costs =

$$\frac{\text{Net cash flow from operating activities} + \text{Interest expense} + \text{Estimated lease interest expense}}{\text{Interest expense} + \text{Estimated lease interest expense}}$$

Net cash flow from operating activities = $100,000 + $10,000 = $110,000

Cash flow coverage of financial fixed costs = $\dfrac{\$110,000 + \$20,000 + \$5,000}{\$20,000 + \$5,000}$

= 5.4×

See LOS 27i

STUDY GUIDANCE

Corporate Finance

This guidance aims to identify the topics that we consider to be of premium importance for your exam preparation.

Study session 11 (Volume 4) comprises of:

Reading 36   Capital Budgeting

Reading 37   Cost of Capital

Reading 38   Measures of Leverage

Reading 39   Dividends and Share Repurchase: Basics

Reading 40   Working Capital Management

Reading 41   Corporate Governance of Listed Companies: A Manual for Investors

Recommended study time is 16 hours of work. An additional 2 hours should be added to complete Progress Test 5.

 Exam focus

This section represents approximately 8% of the exam. Some of the concepts are extensions of work done previously in financial statements analysis and the asset classes. With this in mind it is worth focusing on the key points and not allocating more time than you need to this section.

 Pre-requisites

Basic quantitative applications (study session 2) and financial statements analysis (study session 8) should have been studied. If you have already studied equity and fixed income you will find this easier.

Importance level

High

Key areas

- Capital budgeting process
- Investment decision criteria

Content review – CFA curriculum

Section 2 Capital Budgeting Process (page 6)

Section 3 Basic Principles of Capital Budgeting (page 8)

Read through these two sections carefully making sure you understand the terms in bold.

Section 4 Investment Decision Criteria (pages 10-27)

Some of this section should be revision from previous work (Reading 6 on NPV and IRR) but it is worth reading through these sections again in particular to understand how they relate to projects.

2 hours

The whole of this section is important to read and you should work through the examples attempting to solve the questions and then comparing to the answers. Each subsection (4.1-4.10) is important and may be examined. It is important to focus as much on the issues surrounding the investment criteria and the advantages / disadvantages of the various approaches as the actual calculations themselves. For example, the NPV profile graph is frequently tested.

The summary starting on page 27 is a useful revision guide and is worth reading through quickly before attempting the questions.

Question practice

- There are 18 questions all of which are in exam format starting on page 29. It is worth attempting all of them. It might be worthwhile to attempt every other one now and the rest perhaps when you have finished all the Corporate Finance readings in this study session.

2 hours

- In addition, all questions in the BPP Question Bank should be attempted prior to the exam.

STUDY SESSION 11 – READING 37

Cost of Capital (page 37)

4 hours

Importance level

High

Key areas

- Weighted average cost of capital
- Costing different sources of capital including the impact of taxation

Content review – CFA curriculum

Section 2 Cost of Capital (page 38)

It is important to understand the calculations involved in calculating the weighted average cost of capital and the impact taxation plays (section 2.1, page 39). You need to read through all of section 2 and it is worth doing example 3 on page 41.

Section 3 Costs of the Different Sources of Capital (page 44)

Section 3.1 Cost of Debt (pages 44-47)

This section is a reminder of how to calculate bond yields and if you have understood this previously it should be possible to go through this section quickly.

Section 3.2 Cost of Preferred Stock (pages 47-48)

Also a concept covered previously and it should be possible to read through this section quickly.

2 hours

Section 3.3 Cost of Common Equity (pages 48-54)

Once again this topic is not new, however it is worth reading through this section more carefully. It acts as good revision for equity valuations and you need to understand how the valuation formulas translate into a cost of capital. Also look at section 3.3.3 on page 54, the bond yield plus premium approach.

Section 4 Topics in Cost of Capital Estimation (pages 54-70)

Section 4.1 is found difficult by most students and is considered less key by BPP. At most you need only glance over the concepts in this section. Understand what is meant by country risk but it is more important to understand the use of marginal cost of capital and the correct treatment of floatation costs.

It is not necessary to read the summary.

Question practice

- Attempt questions 1 to 12 (pages 71-73) and 23 to 27 (pages 76-78) for the closest examples of exam standard questions.
- In addition, all questions in the BPP Question Bank should be attempted prior to the exam.

2 hours

STUDY SESSION 11 – READING 38

Measures of Leverage (page 83)

2 hours

Key areas

- There are no real key individual areas in this section. The key thing is to understand what is meant by leverage in general terms and the impact leverage has on a company's returns.

Content review – CFA curriculum

You can read through most of this chapter quite quickly. The important things to understand are the definitions of the various sorts of risk and how these are impacted by leverage. You do not need to work through the examples.

Read the summary on page 105 as well. This is short and covers the few important definitions in the chapter.

1 hour

Question practice

- Attempt all 16 practice problems at the back of this reading on page 107.

- In addition, all questions in the BPP Question Bank should be attempted prior to the exam.

1 hour

Key areas

- Dividends
- Share repurchases

Content review – CFA curriculum

Section 2 Dividends: Forms (pages 114-122)

You should read through this section making sure you understand what is meant by the various terms. It is important to understand the effects of stock dividends as illustrated in exhibit 2 (page 119) and the effect of stock splits as illustrated in exhibit 3 (page 120).

Section 3 Dividends: Payment Chronology (pages 122-125)

This section can be read through quickly and it is not necessary to go through the examples.

Section 4 Share Repurchases (pages 125-134)

1.5 hours

You need to understand the different ways companies can buy back shares but more important is the financial statement effects described in section 4.2.

Section 4.2 Financial Statement Effects of Repurchases (page 128)

Read through this section carefully and work through examples 6, 7 and 8.

Section 4.3 Valuation Equivalence (page 132)

This section can be read through very quickly alongside the concluding remarks.

The summary on pages 134-5 is a useful revision guide worth looking at.

Question practice

- Attempt all 16 questions at the back of this reading starting on page 137 as they are all in exam format. It is worth attempting all of them.

1 hour

- In addition, all questions in the BPP Question Bank should be attempted prior to the exam.

STUDY SESSION 11 – READING 40

Working Capital Management (page 143)

2 hours

Key areas

A lot of the areas in this section were covered in a different context within Reading 28 in the financial reporting and analysis study sessions.

- Liquidity

Content review – CFA curriculum

Section 2 Managing and Measuring Liquidity (pages 145-152)

Although it is an important section it should be possible to read through this section quite quickly. All the ratios have been covered previously. The key thing to understand is what are the positive and negative influences on a company's liquidity and how the financial ratios help highlight these.

Section 3 Managing the Cash Position (pages 152-155)

This section can be read through quickly.

Section 4 Investing Short-term Funds (pages 156-162)

1 hour

Virtually all this section has been covered elsewhere in the syllabus and it is not necessary to do more than glance at this section.

Sections 5-8 Managing Receivables, Payables and Inventory (pages 163-182)

These sections are not key. Some concepts have been covered in the financial statement analysis readings (especially Reading 28) and some parts should be common sense. It is only worth looking quickly through these sections picking out terms in bold and understanding their meaning.

The summary on pages 182-3 adds little value so only needs a quick review.

Question practice

- Attempt all 12 questions at the back of this reading starting on page 184.

- In addition, all questions in the BPP Question Bank should be attempted prior to the exam.

1 hour

STUDY SESSION 11 – READING 41

Corporate Governance of Listed Companies: A Manual for Investors
(page 191)

1.5 hours

Key areas

- Understand examples of good and bad corporate governance

Content review – CFA curriculum

The reading is long (pages 191-230) and extremely factual. We consider also it has limited examinability.

It is recommended that you only read the summary corporate governance considerations regarding the board, management and shareowner rights (pages 197-200). The rest of the reading can be classed as lower priority reference material.

1 hour

Question practice

- There are 4 questions all of which are in exam format on page 231. It is worth attempting all of them.

- In addition, all questions in the BPP Question Bank should be attempted prior to the exam.

30 minutes

CHECKPOINT – END OF STUDY SESSION 11

You are now able to attempt **Progress Test 5 on Corporate Finance**.

2 hours

BPP
LEARNING MEDIA

Progress Test 5 – Corporate Finance

Questions

1. Which of the following is *least likely* to be a major factor that enables a board to exercise its duty to act in the best long-term interests of stakeholders?

   A. Independence.

   B. Experience.

   C. Professional qualifications.

2. A project involves investing $15,000 and receiving $2,000 a year at the end of each year for 20 years. Which of the following is *closest to* the discounted payback period and the net present value, assuming a discount rate of 6%?

	NPV	DISCOUNTED PAYBACK
A.	$7,940	9 years
B.	$7,940	11 years
C.	$8,010	9 years

3. A company has in issue bonds with a par value of $10m which were issued two years ago at a price of 95. The current price is 90. The annual coupon level is 8% and there are five years to maturity. If the tax rate is 30%, the cost of the debt finance is *closest to*:

   A. 5.6%.

   B. 6.3%.

   C. 7.5%.

4. A company has incurred research costs of $300,000 during the last year developing a new product. It is now planning to manufacture this product in a factory which cost $500,000 ten years ago and could now be sold for $900,000. The product will be sold for the next five years, with the following annual profit details.

Sales revenue	$700,000
Direct costs	$350,000
Fixed overheads	$50,000

   The fixed overheads cost is the reallocation of existing head office expenditure that is incurred regardless of whether this project is undertaken.

   The internal rate of return of the project is *closest to*:

   A. 14.1%.

   B. 19.9%.

   C. 27.2%.

5.   Which of the following statements regarding corporate governance is *most accurate*?

   I   Takeover defences will increase the value of a share

   II   If only some shareholders are entitled to vote, management may focus on the interests of those shareholders

	STATEMENT I	STATEMENT II
A.	Incorrect	Correct
B.	Correct	Incorrect
C.	Incorrect	Incorrect

6.   Which of the following statements regarding the election of board members is *most accurate*?

   A. Annual elections reduce the flexibility of shareowners.

   B. Classified boards provide continuity.

   C. Classified boards are re-elected each year.

7.   XYZ Company has 300,000 bonds outstanding, each with a $2,000 par value, and a current price of $1,850. The company also has 10 million shares of common stock outstanding with a current price of $82 each, and a book value of $100 each. The capital structure is not expected to change in the future. What weights for debt and equity should the firm use to calculate its weighted average cost of capital?

	EQUITY	DEBT
A.	62.5%	37.5%
B.	59.6%	40.4%
C.	37.5%	62.5%

8.   In which of the following cases would the IRR approach give the same result as the NPV method?

   A. Comparing mutually exclusive projects.

   B. Evaluating a project with multiple yields.

   C. Evaluating an independent project.

9.   Yves Inc. is appraising a project which involves initial cash outflows of $35,000 with inflows each year of $10,000 for five years, starting at the end of the first year. Yves Inc.'s cost of capital is 12%. Should the company accept the project?

   A. The project has a net present value of $1,048 and should be rejected.

   B. The project has a net present value of $1,048 and should be accepted.

   C. The project has a net present value of $36,048 and should be accepted.

10.   Which of the following would cause a company's WACC to rise?

   A. A decrease in expected inflation.

   B. A decrease in tax rate.

   C. A decrease in interest rates.

11. Which of the following statements is correct?

    A. The value of irredeemable debt is the present value of the future interest payments on the instrument, discounted at the debt investor's required rate of return.

    B. New investment should be appraised by reference to the cost of the finance raised to finance that particular investment.

    C. Conglomerates should use one Weighted Average Cost of Capital to appraise new investment by all divisions.

12. The start-up of a project will involve a building and two materials, A and B. The building originally cost $500,000 to buy and could be sold now for $600,000. If material A is not used in this project, it will have to be disposed of at a cost of $40,000. If material B is not used in this project, it could be sold for $30,000 or used in another project with a net present value of $35,000. No more material B is available.

    The project has involved marketing and research to date costing $8,000. This is to be paid in the near future. In addition, it will involve the purchase of a temporary warehouse costing $40,000. This will eventually be sold for $30,000.

    The initial incremental investment outlay for the project is *closest to*:

    A. $605,000.

    B. $613,000.

    C. $635,000.

13. A company has $600,000 par value of irredeemable debt in issue with an annual coupon of 8% and a price of 98. It also has 100,000 $1 nominal value common stock in issue with a price of $10. The dividend in one year's time is $0.20, the growth rate in dividends is 5% and the tax rate is 30%. The company's WACC is *closest to*:

    A. 4.22%.

    B. 5.89%.

    C. 6.52%.

14. A bond is priced at 105 and has an annual 9% coupon. It is redeemable in three years. The federal tax rate is 30% and the state tax rate is 5%. The cost of debt is *closest to*:

    A. 4.6%.

    B. 5.0%.

    C. 5.4%.

15. Which of the following components of a company's executive compensation program is *most likely* to negatively affect shareowners' interests?

    A. Share ownership of management.

    B. Bonus schemes.

    C. Option repricing.

16. A company's operating profit increases by 40% when the sales increase by 10%. The degree of financial leverage is 3×. How much will net income increase by if sales increase by 5%?

    A. + 20%.

    B. + 7%.

    C. + 60%.

17. Fly Away Inc is a listed travel agency that was founded twenty years ago by David Knott. Although David floated the business five years ago, he still serves as the Chairman of the Board. The remainder of the Board is made up of a mixture of employees and non-executive directors. The CEO of the company also sits on the Board. Which of the following is *most likely* to indicate that the Board is not fully independent?

    A. The presence of employees on the Board.

    B. The presence of the CEO on the Board.

    C. David Knott being the Chair of the Board.

18. Whenever the NPV of a project is positive, the profitability index will be:

    A. Greater than 1.0.

    B. Between 0 and 1.

    C. Equal to 1.0.

19. An analyst makes the following estimates for a capital investment project:

    Price   = $100 per unit

    Variable costs   = $50 per unit

    Cash fixed costs = $10,000

    Depreciation   = $2,000

    The breakeven quantity of sales is closest to:

    A. 100 units.

    B. 200 units.

    C. 240 units.

20. A project has the following cash flows.

	$
Time 0	588
Time 1	(1,440)
Time 2	864

The project has IRRs of 5% and 40%. At what discount rates should it be accepted?

A. Less than 5%.

B. 5% to 40%.

C. Less than 5% and more than 40%.

21. The following details are extracted from a company's balance sheet.

	$000
Current assets	500
Noncurrent assets	600
	1,100
Liabilities	300
Debt – 5% coupon	200
Stakeholders' equity	600
	1,100

The earnings per share for the year just ended is $2 and the dividend payout ratio is 40%. There are 100,000 shares in issue with a market price of $30. The required return of debt investors is 5%. The debt was issued and is redeemable at par. The tax rate is 40%.

The company's WACC is *closest to*:

A. 21%.

B. 22%.

C. 23%.

22. ABC Corporation is considering an investment of $750 million with expected after-tax cash inflows of $175 million per year for seven years. The required rate of return is 10 percent. Expressed in years, what is the project's:

	PAYBACK PERIOD?	DISCOUNTED PAYBACK PERIOD?
A.	4.3	5.4
B.	4.3	5.9
C.	4.8	5.4

CFA Level I ◆ Progress Test 5 – Questions

23. An investment of $20,000 will create a perpetual after-tax cash flow of $2,000. The required rate of return is 8 percent. The investment's profitability index is *closest to*:

   A. 1.25.

   B. 1.16.

   C. 1.08.

24. Jonathan Ward is reviewing a profitable investment project that has a conventional cash flow pattern (initial cash outflow followed by cash inflows). If the initial outlay and future after-tax cash flows all triple for the project, what would Ward predict for:

	IRR?	NPV?
A.	Increase	Increase
B.	Increase	Stay the same
C.	Stay the same	Increase

25. Barbara Donnelly has evaluated an investment project and found that its payback period is one year, its NPV is negative, and its IRR is positive. Is this combination of results possible?

   A. Yes.

   B. No, because a project with a positive IRR has a positive NPV.

   C. No, because a project with a negative NPV has a negative payback period.

26. An investment has an outlay of $200 and after-tax cash flows of $60 at the end of each year for the next four years. A further investment increases the outlay by $30 and the annual after-tax cash flows by $18. As a result, what happens to the:

	VERTICAL INTERCEPT OF THE NPV PROFILE?	HORIZONTAL INTERCEPT OF THE NPV PROFILE?
A.	Shifts up	Shifts left
B.	Shifts up	Shifts right
C.	Shifts down	Shifts left

27. Gamma corporation wishes to maintain a debt: equity ratio of 1.3. The company can raise £3m of debt before increasing the cost of debt. It can use £2m of equity from retained earnings before increasing the cost of equity. What is closest to the company's break point?

   A. £2m.

   B. £2.67.

   C. £3m.

28. The cost of equity capital is equal to the:

   A. Expected market return.

   B. Rate of return required by stockholders.

   C. Cost of retained earnings plus dividends.

29. An insurance company will pay a dividend of $2.30 next year with a payout ratio of 30 percent. The current stock price is $45 and return on equity is 15 percent. Using the dividend discount model, the cost of equity capital for the company is *closest to*:

   A. 9.61 percent.

   B. 10.50 percent.

   C. 15.61 percent.

30. Delta Construction issued a fixed-rate perpetual preferred stock five years ago. The preferred stock is noncallable and nonconvertible. The stock was issued at $25 per share with a $1.75 dividend. If the company were to issue preferred stock today, the yield would be 6.5 percent. Delta's marginal tax rate is 40 percent. The stock's current value is *closest to*:

   A. $25.00.

   B. $26.92.

   C. $41.67.

Progress Test 5 – Corporate Finance

Answers

1. **C** Professional qualifications is not correct because this is just one consideration in evaluating the overall experience and expertise of board members

   See LOS 41b

2. **B** Using your cash flow function:

   CF0 = – 15,000

   C01 = 2,000

   F01 = 20

   NPV = 7,940

   To see if the discounted payback is 9 or 11 years, try F01 = 9 and F01 = 11.

   The NPV is negative when F01 = 9 but turns positive for F01 = 11. To double check this, the NPV is still negative when F01 = 10, so the payback must turn positive in the 11th year.

   Alternatively, if you have the Texas BA11 Plus Professional Model, press the down arrow three times after the NPV calculation and you will see the DPB = 10.27 years. As the cash flow is at the end of each year, we have to round up to 11 years

   See LOS 36d

3. **C** The pre-tax cost of debt is calculated at 10.684% using your IRR function. Multiply by (1–Tax rate) to work out the after tax cost of debt.

   10.684% × (1 − 0.3) = 7.48%

   Remember to use the current yield on the company's bonds, not the coupon rate, or yield on issue

   See LOS 37f

4. **C** N = 5

   PV = – 900

   PMT = 350

   CPT I/Y = 27.2%

   The research costs are sunk. The opportunity cost of using the factory is 900,000. The fixed overheads are ignored as they are not incremental

   See LOS 36d

5. **A** Takeover defenses may make otherwise attractive bids less likely to succeed, reducing share value

   See LOS 41g

6. **B** A classified board consists of board members that are elected for staggered multiple year terms, providing more continuity to the board structure

   See LOS 41b

7. **B**   The WACC is calculated using the market value of debt and equity

	$ m	%
Debt value	555	40.4
Equity value	820	59.6
	1,375	100.0

See LOS 37a

8. **C**   When comparing projects that are mutually exclusive, NPV is always the preferred method. When there are changes in the cash flow directions, the IRR approach may result in multiple IRRs, in which case we have to revert to the NPV approach

See LOS 36e

9. **B**   CFO = – 35,000

COI = 5,000

FOI = 5

CPT NPV = +1,048

Since the project has a positive net present value, it should be accepted

See LOS 36d

10. **B**   A reduction in the tax rate will increase the net cost of debt to the company

See LOS 37a

11. **A**   B is incorrect as the discount rate should be based on all finance rather than just an incremental amount, and WACC can be adjusted for the risk exposure, through β, making C incorrect

See LOS 37a

12. **C**

	$
Building	600,000
Material A	(40,000)
Material B	35,000
Warehouse	40,000
	635,000

Note that the marketing and research is a sunk cost and therefore should not be included in the incremental investment outlay calculation

See LOS 36b

13. **C** $r_d (1 - t) = \dfrac{8}{98} \times (1 - 30\%) = 5.71\%$

$r_e = \dfrac{\$0.20}{\$10} + 5\% = 7\%$

Total value of debt = $600,000 \times 0.98 = \$588,000$

Total value of equity = $100,000 \times \$10 = \$1,000,000$

WACC $= 5.71\% \times \dfrac{588}{1,588} + 7\% \times \dfrac{1,000}{1,588}$

$= 6.52\%$

See LOS 37a

14. **A**

Time	Flow
0	(1,050)
1	90
2	90
3	1,090

Use your calculator to compute the IRR of the cash flows (IRR = 7.1%)

$k_d = 7.1\% \times (1 - 0.35) = 4.6\%$, both tax rates added together to give the investor's total tax rate

See LOS 37f

15. **C**   Option repricing removes the original long-term goal set for management

See LOS 41b

16. **C**   The operating leverage is 4× and the financial leverage is 3×. Therefore the total leverage is 12×. A 5% increase in sales will lead to a 60% increase in net income

See LOS 38a

17. **C**   Employees being on the Board only indicates a lack of independence if they are the majority. Similarly, the CEO being on the Board only indicates a lack of independence if they are also the Chair

See LOS 41b

18. **A**   The profitability index $= 1 + \dfrac{NPV}{CFO}$, indicating a positive NPV if it is >1

See LOS 36d

19.   **C**   The formula for the accounting breakeven is

      Q = F/(P - V)

      Where   Q = total units sold
              F = fixed costs including depreciation
              P = selling price per unit
              V = variable cost per unit

      Therefore,

      Q   = 10,000 + 2,000)/(100 – 50)
           = 12,000/50
           = 250 units

      See LOS 38d

20.   **C**   The project has a NPV of $12 at a discount rate of zero, ascertained by adding the undiscounted cash flows to get the vertical intercept. This tells us that the NPV is positive between zero and the first IRR of 5%, and again beyond the second IRR of 40%

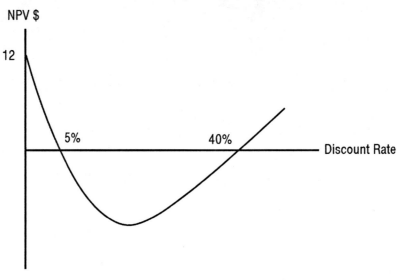

      See LOS 36d

21. **B** $WACC = k_d \times w_d + k_e \times w_e$

Where $k_e = D_1/P + g$ and $g = ROE \times b$

(and ROE = (Net income or earnings)/Equity = (Earnings per share $\times$ No. of shares issued)/Equity = $(2 \times 100,000)/600,000 = 33\%$)

(and $b = 1 -$ Payout ratio $= 1 - 0.4 = 0.6$)

Hence $g = 33 \times 0.6 = 20\%$

and $D_1 = D_0 \times (1 + g) =$ Earnings $\times$ Payout ratio $\times (1 + g) = 2 \times 0.4 \times (1 + 0.2) = 0.96$

Hence $k_e = 0.96/30 + 0.2 = 0.232$ (23.2%)

$K_d = 5\% \times (1 - 0.4) = 3\%$

We use the current yield on the debt, adjusted for tax

$w_e =$ Equity funding/(Equity funding + Debt funding) all at market prices

$= 100,000 \times 30/(100,000 \times 30 + 200,000 \times 1) = 3.0/3.2$

(30 is market price of equity and the bonds are trading at par)

$w_d =$ Debt/(Equity + Debt) $= 0.2/3.2$

Therefore, WACC $= 0.2/3.2 \times 3 + 3.0/3.2 \times 23.2 = 21.94\%$

See LOS 37a

22. **B**   The payback period is between four and five years. Precisely, the payback period is four years plus $50 / $175 = 0.29 of the fifth year cash flow, or 4.29 years.

The discounted payback period is between five and six years. After five years, the discounted present value of the project's cash inflows amounts to $663.39. This payback period is five years plus $86.61 / $98.78 = 0.88 of the sixth year cash flow, or 5.88 years

Alternatively, using the Texas BA11 Plus Professional, you can enter the cash flows and scroll down after the NPV for the PB (payback) and the PDB (discounted payback)

See LOS 36d

23. **A**   The PV of the future cash flows = $2,000 / 0.08 = $25,000

The profitability index (PI) = PV / Investment = $25,000 / $20,000 = 1.25

See LOS 36d

24. **C**   IRR would stay the same because the return on each dollar invested would be the same. As all of the cash flows and their present values would triple, then the difference between the sum of the PVs and the initial outlay would also triple

See LOS 36d

25. **A**   If the cumulative cash flow in the first year is equal to the initial outlay, then this would give a payback period of one year. If subsequent cash flows are comparatively small, then NPV could be negative, while IRR could be positive, albeit below the discount rate

See LOS 36d and e

26.   **B**   The vertical intercept showing NPV increases from 40 to 82, while the horizontal intercept showing the IRR rate increases from 7.7% to 13.4%

        See LOS 36e

27.   **B**   The break point represents the total amount of finance that can be raised without increasing the WACC. Debt is 25% of the total finance and equity is 75%

        The debt break point is $\dfrac{£3m}{0.25}$ = £12m

        The equity break point is $\dfrac{£2m}{0.75}$ = £2.67m

        The first break point is therefore at £2.67m

        See LOS 36e

28.   **B**   Note that the cost of equity can be estimated using the CAPM, dividend discount model and bond yield plus risk premium approaches

        See LOS 37h

29.   **C**   First calculate the sustainable growth rate of the company:

        g = (1 – dividend payout ratio) × (ROE) = (1 – 0.30) × (15%) = 10.5%

        Rearranging the DDM equation:

        r_e = (D_1 / P_0) + g = ($2.30 / $45) + 10.50% = 15.61%

        See LOS 37h

30.   **B**   As the company can issue new preferred stock at 6.5%, then

        P_p = $1.75 / 0.065 = $26.92

        As dividends on preferred stock are not tax deductible, there is no adjustment for taxes

        See LOS 37g

STUDY GUIDANCE

Portfolio Management

This guidance aims to identify the topics that we consider to be of premium importance for your exam preparation.

Study session 12 (Volume 4) comprises of:

Reading 42   Portfolio Management: An Overview

Reading 43   Portfolio Risk and Return: Part I

Reading 44   Portfolio Risk and Return: Part II

Reading 45   Basics of Portfolio Planning and Construction

Recommended study time is 13.5 hours of work. An additional 2 hours should be added to complete Progress Test 6 on Portfolio Management.

 ## Exam focus

This section represents approximately 5% of the exam. With this in mind it is worth focusing on the key points and not allocating more time than you need to this section. Do ensure that all steps towards the final conclusions are covered, as exam questions can come from any point in the theory leading up to the Capital Asset Pricing Model.

 ## Pre-requisites

Basic quantitative applications (study session 2) should be studied before attempting this study session.

Key areas

- Objectives and investment constraints
- Portfolio management process

Content review – CFA curriculum

This reading is largely factual and it is not necessary to go through the whole chapter in detail.

Section 2 Portfolio Perspective on Investing (pages 237-246)

This is an introductory section and you can read through it quite quickly without spending much time on the exhibits.

Section 3 Investment Clients (pages 246-253)

You only need to know in broad terms the different sort of clients so you only need read the definitions of the investors and do not need to go into any detail.

1 hour

Section 4 Steps in the Portfolio Management Process (pages 253-257)

This section is of more importance. You need to know the steps involved in making portfolio management decisions and the order that they come in.

Section 5 Pooled Investments (pages 257-268)

This section is largely non-key although you may want to look briefly at the different types of mutual funds. A section worth reading in detail is 5.3.3 (page 266) the section on hedge funds. Make sure you understand what different hedge funds do and what strategies they follow.

The summary adds little value, so can be skipped.

Question practice

- There are 15 questions all of which are in exam format starting on page 270. It is worth attempting all of them.

- In addition, all questions in the BPP Question Bank should be attempted prior to the exam.

1 hour

STUDY SESSION 12 – READING 43

Portfolio Risk and Return: Part 1 (page 275)

5 hours

Key areas

This reading along with Reading 44 is a key section. Remember though that it is still a small part of the exam overall. Some of the concepts have been covered in quantitative applications (Study Session 2) already although this section looks at the application of some of the concepts more. If you struggle with the statistics, focus on the key definitions and being able to describe the concepts. In the exam you are unlikely to be asked to do detailed calculations.

- Risk aversion, utility curves
- Diversification
- Efficient frontiers and optimal portfolios

Content review – CFA curriculum

Section 2 Investment Characteristics of Assets (pages 276-299)

This section acts a reminder of statistical concepts already covered. Spend the necessary time going through this section if you cannot remember the concepts from before. If you can, then you can go through it a bit quicker.

A new concept is the variance of a portfolio of assets in section 2.3 (page 288) It is worth looking at this in detail focusing on the concept as much as the calculation.

Sections such as historical return and risk (section 2.4 pages 291-299) can be gone through very quickly.

Section 3 Risk Aversion and Portfolio Selection (pages 299-308)

This section covers a number of important areas. Do not focus on the more complex statistics in the text, focus on the concepts and the easier calculations. You must understand the concept of utility curves and indifference curves. Example 5 on page 303 is a good example to work through. Example 6 on page 304 is more complex than you would find in the exam.

Having understood the concept of indifference curves you need to also understand how these apply to portfolio selection. Do not worry about understanding the statistical formulae just the concepts as illustrated in the graphs.

3 hours

Section 4 Portfolio Risk (pages 308-320)

Once again focus on the concepts rather than the detailed mathematics. Focus on the concept of diversification and its benefits. If you do this then you will be able to read through this section relatively quickly.

Section 5 Efficient Frontier and Investor's Optimal Portfolio (pages 320-331)

This is another section which a lot of students find difficult. Understand what is meant by the investment opportunity set and how different portfolios relate to each other leading to the efficient frontier. You need also to understand what happens with the introduction of a risk free asset and the capital allocation line. You do not need to go beyond section 5.3 (ending page 326). The remainder of the chapter contains comprehensive examples which are far more complicated than you will face in the exam.

The summary on page 332 is a useful quick revision guide.

Question practice

- There are 40 questions all of which are in exam format and they begin on page 333. It is worth attempting all of them. It might be worthwhile to attempt every other one now and the rest perhaps when you have finished all the Corporate Finance section. Alternatively leave some for final revision practice.

2 hours

- In addition, all questions in the BPP Question Bank should be attempted prior to the exam.

Key areas

Focus on the definitions and concepts rather than detailed calculations.

This section is a follow on from Reading 43.

- Risk free asset
- Capital allocation line
- Capital asset pricing model
- Security market line

Content review – CFA curriculum

The text is very detailed and some students struggle to understand the concepts because of the depth gone into.

Section 2 Capital Market Theory (pages 346-358)

You need to read through this section from the beginning. You should make sure that you understand exhibit 1 on page 348. The concept is illustrated further in exhibit 2 on the following page.

Section 2.1.2 is of less importance

Focus on understanding what is meant by 'the market' in section 2.2.2 (page 351) and what is meant by the capital market line. If the mathematics is confusing, do not spend any time trying to understand it. Exhibit 3 (page 352) is a demonstration of the capital market line concept. Try to do example 1 question 1 (page 353), you need not attempt question 2.

You will also need to understand what is meant by leverage and how this can impact the capital market line. Once again the greatest focus should be on the concept and the diagrammatic illustrations rather than the detailed calculations. Example 2 (page 355) is a good test of your understanding of the mathematical side and if possible you should attempt it. It is far more detailed than you would get in the exam.

3 hours

Section 3 Pricing of Risk and Computation of Expected Return (page 358)

This section introduces the idea of systematic and non-systematic risk. This area has been examined regularly in the past. You also need to understand what is meant by beta as this is a key component in the capital asset pricing model (CAPM). Try to understand the single index model used to calculate beta, but more important is the calculation and interpretation of beta.

Section 3.2.6 (page 365), beta and expected return is a key section. If you understand this the rest of the reading will be a lot easier. It is worth working through example 6 (page 366) to cement your understanding.

Section 4 The Capital Asset Pricing Model (page 367)

Understand the assumptions behind CAPM but you do not need to read all the text.

A key concept is the security market line which a lot of students get confused with the capital market line. You will need to read through most of section 4 carefully. Try to solve the questions in examples 8 (page 371) and 9 (page 373) but you do not need to attempt examples 10 and 11 which are overly long and detailed.

It is important to understand the concepts represented in exhibits 12 (page 380) and 13 (page 381). These are two concepts which are easier to understand and could be examined.

Section 5 Beyond the Capital Asset Pricing Model (pages 383-386)

This section is non-key and can be read through very quickly.

The summary on page 386 is worth reading at this stage especially given the number of different concepts introduced.

Question practice

- There are 40 questions all of which are in exam format starting on page 388. It is worth attempting all of them. It might be worthwhile to attempt every other one now and the rest perhaps when you have finished all the Corporate Finance section. Alternatively, leave some for final revision practice.

2 hours

- In addition, all the questions in the BPP Question Bank should be attempted prior to the exam.

STUDY SESSION 12 – READING 45

Basics of Portfolio Planning and Construction (page 397)   **1.5 hours**

Key areas

- Investment policy statement

Content review – CFA curriculum

This reading is primarily factual and to some extent should be common sense to most students as some of it ties in with the ethical standards.

If you read sections 2.1 (page 398), 2.2 (page 399) and the summary (page 428) you will have covered the key points. Given time constraints the rest of the reading can be ignored, other than to refer to if required when attempting questions.

30 minutes

Question practice

- There are 20 questions all of which are in exam format starting on page 430. You should attempt them all.

- In addition, all questions in the BPP Question Bank should be attempted prior to the exam.

1 hour

CHECKPOINT – END OF STUDY SESSION 12

You are now able to attempt the **Progress Test 6 on Portfolio Management**.

2 hours

Progress Test 6 – Portfolio Management

Questions

1. When estimating a security's beta from its characteristic line, which of the following is *least likely* to affect the value of the estimated beta?

    A. The time interval.

    B. The alpha factor.

    C. The market proxy.

2. Which of the following *most accurately* describes the change in the SML if there is an increase in risk tolerance for risky stocks, all other things being equal?

    A. The gradient of the SML increases.

    B. There is a parallel shift downwards of the SML.

    C. The gradient of the SML decreases.

3. The capital market line depicts the required return from:

    A. A security given its level of systematic risk, as measured in standard deviations.

    B. A security given its level of systematic risk, as measured by beta.

    C. A combination of a risk-free asset and the risky market portfolio given the risk of the combined portfolio, measured in standard deviations.

4. A stock has a beta of 0.5, the risk-free rate of return is 7% and the market risk premium is 8%. The stock is estimated to earn a return of 10%. Which of the following statements is *most accurate*?

    A. The stock has overperformed.

    B. The stock has underperformed.

    C. The stock has performed as expected.

5. The correlation coefficient between the risk-free asset and all other risky assets is equal to:

    A. −1.0

    B. 0.0

    C. +1.0

6. An investment has an expected return of 10% and a risk in standard deviations of 6%. Another investment has an expected return of 6% and a risk in standard deviations of zero. The correlation coefficient of returns between the two investments is zero. The expected standard deviation of an equally weighted portfolio containing both investments is *closest to*:

    A. 0%.

    B. 3%.

    C. 8%.

7. Which of the following would be the *least appropriate* investment for an individual investor paying income tax at high rates?

   A. Exchange traded fund.

   B. High growth equities.

   C. High yield bonds.

8. Which of the following lines showing the possible risks and returns available from possible combinations of investments A and B gives the highest positive correlation between investments A and B?

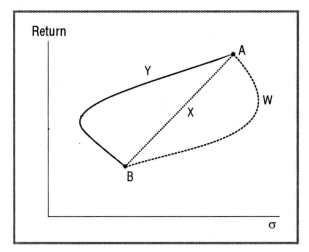

   A. W

   B. X

   C. Y

9. Which of the three available answers could represent the lowest possible risk that could be achieved from combining the following two imperfectly negatively correlated investments?

Investment	A	B
Return	10%	12%
Risk	4%	5%

   A. 0%.

   B. 3%.

   C. 4%.

10. An investment has a covariance with the market portfolio of 150. The market portfolio risk is 10% and the market return is 12%. If the risk-free return is 5%, the return that may be expected from the investment is *closest to*:

   A. 15.5%.

   B. 13.5%.

   C. 12.0%.

11. Stocks A, B and C each have the same expected return and standard deviation. The following table shows the correlations between the returns on these stocks.

Correlation of Stock Returns			
	Stock A	Stock B	Stock C
Stock A	+1.0		
Stock B	+0.9	+1.0	
Stock C	+1.0	−0.4	+1.0

Given these correlations, the portfolio constructed from these stocks having the *lowest risk* is a portfolio:

A. Invested in stocks A and B.

B. Invested in stocks A and C.

C. Invested in stocks B and C.

12. The correlation coefficient of Portfolio X's returns and the markets returns is 0.95, and the correlation coefficient of Portfolio Y's returns and the market's returns is 0.60. Both portfolios have a beta coefficient equal to 1.0. Which of the following statements *best describes* the levels of portfolio diversification?

A. Both Portfolio X and Portfolio Y are well diversified.

B. Both Portfolio X and Portfolio Y are poorly diversified.

C. Portfolio X is well diversified and Portfolio Y is poorly diversified.

13. A risk-averse investor owning stock in White Corporation decides to add the stock of either Black Corporation or Green Corporation to her portfolio. All three stocks offer the same expected return and total risk. The covariance of returns between White stock and Black stock is −0.05 and White stock and Green stock is +0.05. Portfolio risk is expected to:

A. Decline more by buying Black Corporation.

B. Decline more by buying Green Corporation.

C. Increase by buying either Black or Green Corporation.

14. According to the capital asset pricing model, the rate of return of a portfolio with a beta of 1.2, given a market risk premium of 6.5 percent while the risk-free rate of 5 percent is:

A. 12.8%.

B. 12.5%.

C. 11.5 %.

15. How can an investor achieve returns greater on average than those earned by a market portfolio, assuming efficient markets?

A. By varying the beta of his portfolio with changing market conditions.

B. By taking on additional unsystematic risk in his portfolio to increase the expected return from the portfolio.

C. By borrowing money and investing this in the market portfolio.

16. For two investments of equal size, with the following details, which combination would give the lowest risk?

Investment	Expected Return	Risk (Standard Deviation)
A	10%	6%
B	15%	8%

Correlation coefficient between A and B = –1.0

	A	B
A.	0.50	0.50
B.	0.55	0.45
C.	0.57	0.43

17. A negative alpha for a portfolio indicates:

A. An abnormal loss.

B. The portfolio moves in the same direction as the market.

C. The portfolio moves in opposite directions to the market.

18. Which of the following represents the correct ordering of steps in the portfolio management process?

    I   Forecast market conditions

    II   Construct portfolio

    III Create investment policy statement

    IV   Measure performance

A. I, III, II and IV.

B. II, III, IV and I.

C. III, I, II and IV.

19. A portfolio was created by investing 75% of the funds in Investment A and 25% in Investment B. Investment A has a standard deviation of 10% and Investment B has a standard deviation of 15%. The correlation coefficient between A and B is 0.75. The risk of the portfolio is *closest to*:

A. 10.6%.

B. 11.2%.

C. 12.4%.

20. An advisor documents the following investment needs of his client:

    Time horizon: Very long

    Risk tolerance: High

    Income needs: To meet spending commitments

    Liquidity needs: Low

    Which of the following *most closely* describes the adviser's client?
    A. Defined benefit plan.
    B. Endowment.
    C. Bank.

21. The systematic risk on an investment is 7%, the risk of the market portfolio is 9%, the risk-free return is 6% and market risk premium is 8%. The expected return on the investment is *closest to*:
    A. 12%.
    B. 13%.
    C. 14%.

22. Four securities offer the following risks and returns.

	Return	Risk
1	17%	5%
2	18%	4%
3	19%	6%

    Which one of the securities is *least appropriate* for a risk-averse investor?
    A. Security 1.
    B. Security 2.
    C. Security 3.

23. The market risk is 20%, measured in standard deviations and the covariance of the returns of a security and the market is 440. Which of the following is *closest to* the beta of the security?
    A. 1.3
    B. 1.1
    C. 0.9

24. When a stock has a beta of greater than one, this indicates that a stock will:
    A. On average give a return above the yield on the market.
    B. On average give a return below that of a stock with a beta of less than one.
    C. Have a high level of systematic risk relative to total risk.

25. The combination of risk-free borrowing and lending with a risky portfolio is represented by:

    A. CML.

    B. Efficient frontier.

    C. Beta.

26. Changes in which of the following will change the slope of the security market line?

	RISK-FREE RATE	INVESTOR'S RISK AVERSION
A.	Correct	Correct
B.	Correct	Incorrect
C.	Incorrect	Correct

27. A stock that is relatively unaffected by general fluctuations in the economy can be characterized as:

    A. A cyclical stock.

    B. Having a low beta.

    C. Having high unsystematic risk.

28. Given the covariance and standard deviation of two assets, the correlation coefficient is *closest to*:

    Asset A standard deviation = 2.2

    Asset B standard deviation = 0.80

    Covariance = 1.76

    A. −0.36

    B. 0.36

    C. 1.00

29. Which one of the following is *least likely* to be part of development of an investor's policy statement?

    A. Assessment of risk tolerance.

    B. Identification of return objectives.

    C. Fees.

30. Stock A has a beta of 0.6, and is currently priced at $40. Its estimated price at the end of the year is $45. Stock B has a beta of 0.75, and is currently priced at $60. Its estimated price at the end of the year is $65. In addition, Stock B is expected to pay a $2 dividend. The risk-free rate is 5% and the expected market return is 12%.

    Which of the following is *most accurate* with regard to the current stock prices?

	STOCK A	STOCK B
A.	Underpriced	Underpriced
B.	Overpriced	Underpriced
C.	Overpriced	Overpriced

Progress Test 6 – Portfolio Management

Answers

1. **B** The alpha factor is obtained from the regression analysis, and is unrelated to the calculation of beta

    See LOS 44e

2. **C** Investors would be prepared to accept less return for any given level of risk

    See LOS 44f

3. **C** The definition in B is for the security market line

    See LOS 44b

4. **B** Required return = $7 + 0.5 \times 8 = 11\%$. This is greater than the actual return, so the stock has underperformed

    See LOS 44h

5. **B** By definition the correlation coefficient is equal to zero: the risk-free asset is not affected by the risky assets

    See LOS 44a

6. **B** $\sigma = 0.5 \times 6 = 3$

    See LOS 44e

7. **C** Higher income levels give higher taxes

    See LOS 42d and 45e

8. **B** Line X illustrates perfect positive correlation. Line W is not possible for any correlation coefficient

    See LOS 43f

9. **B** Reducing risk to 0% would only be possible with perfect negative correlation. Since Investment A has a risk of 4%, it should be possible to reduce risk below this level, meaning that 3% is the correct answer

    See LOS 43f

10. **A** $\beta = \dfrac{\text{Covariance}}{\text{Variance}_m} = \dfrac{150}{100} = 1.5$

    $r = r_f + \beta(r_m - r_f) = 5 + 1.5\,(12 - 5) = 15.5\%$

    See LOS 44g

11. **C** The more negative the correlation, the greater the diversification benefits

    See LOS 43f

12. **C** A high correlation coefficient indicates that most of the security's total risk is systematic risk. Portfolio Y has a significant amount of unsystematic risk, therefore can not be fully diversified

See LOS 44e

13. **A** The portfolio risk, as measured by the standard deviation, will decline more by buying Black Corporation stock. This is because the covariance of returns between White stock and Black stock (Cov = –0.05) is lower than between White stock and Green stock (Cov = +0.05)

See LOS 43f

14. **A** $E(R_{port})$ = 5% + 1.2(6.5%)

= 12.8%

Be careful here as you are given the market risk premium, which is $R_m - R_f$

See LOS 44g

15. **C** In efficient markets, option A will not be possible. To increase expected returns we need to gear up the portfolio by introducing leverage

See LOS 44b

16. **C** $\sigma_{a,b}^2 = p_a^2\sigma_a^2 + p_b^2\sigma_b^2 + 2p_a p_b \sigma_a \sigma_b cor_{a,b}$

$\sigma_{a,b}^2 = 0.57^2 \times 6^2 + 0.43^2 \times 8^2 + 2 \times 0.57 \times 0.43 \times 6 \times 8 \times (-1)$

$\sigma_{a,b}^2 = NIL$

This question is calculation intensive. It will help if your calculator setting is AOS (see calculator guide) as then you can type the whole variance calculation in one go and save time

See LOS 43e

17. **A** This is when the expected return is less than the required return

See LOS 44h

18. **C** The investment policy statement provides the overall structure to the investment process

See LOS 42c

19. **A** $\sigma_{a,b}^2 = p_a^2\sigma_a^2 + p_b^2\sigma_b^2 + 2p_a p_a \sigma_a \sigma_b cor_{a,b}$

$\sigma_{a,b}^2 = 0.75^2 \times 10^2 + 0.25^2 \times 15^2 + 2 \times 0.75 \times 0.25 \times 10 \times 15 \times 0.75$

= 112.5

$\sigma_{a,b} = 10.6\%$

See LOS 43e

20. **B** Income needs for pension plans can be high or low depending on the maturity of the fund. Banks tend to have a short horizon, low risk tolerance and high liquidity needs

See LOS 42b

21.   **A**   Return $= 6 + \dfrac{7}{9} \times 8 = 12.2\%$

         See LOS 44g

22.   **A**   Security 1 is dominated by Security 2 as it has a lower expected return for higher risk

         See LOS 43d

23.   **B** $\beta = \dfrac{\text{Covariance}(i,m)}{\text{Variance of market}}$

         $\beta = \dfrac{440}{20^2}$

         $\beta = 1.1$

         See LOS 44e

24.   **A**   The market by definition has a beta of 1. We cannot conclude about the level of unsystematic v systematic risk

         See LOS 44e

25.   **A**   The ability to lend and borrow at the risk-free rate when combined with a risky portfolio results in the capital market line (CML)

         See LOS 44b

26.   **C**   The slope of the SML is the value of the market risk premium (Market return – Risk-free rate) and is determined by the level of risk aversion in the market. The steeper the line, the higher the level of risk aversion. Interest rate changes (risk-free or market rates) impact the SML by shifting the line up or down rather than changing its slope, because change in the risk-free rate will, all things being equal, result in an equivalent change in the market return, keeping the risk premium constant

         See LOS 44f

27.   **B**   Stocks that are relatively unaffected by economic fluctuations decline during down markets, but not as much as the overall market. A stock that moves in a similar fashion to the market, but without large swings in their rates of return, have low systematic risk as measured by beta

         See LOS 44e

28.   **C** $\text{Cor}_{AB} = \dfrac{\text{Covariance}_{(A,B)}}{\sigma_A \times \sigma_B}$

         $= \dfrac{1.76}{2.2 \times 0.80} = 1.0$

         See LOS 43b

29.   **C**   The policy statement contains details of the investor's objectives and constraints

         See LOS 45b

30.   A   **Stock A**

Estimated return = $\dfrac{5}{40} \times 100 = 12.5\%$

CAPM expected return = $5 + 0.6\,(12 - 5)$

$= 9.2\%$

Therefore Stock A is underpriced

Stock B

Estimated return = $\dfrac{(5+2)}{60} \times 100 = 11.7\%$

CAPM expected return = $5 + 0.75\,(12 - 5)$

$= 10.3\%$

Therefore Stock B is underpriced

See LOS 44h

STUDY GUIDANCE

Equity: Market Organization, Market Indices, and Market Efficiency

This guidance aims to identify the topics that we consider to be of premium importance for your exam preparation.

Study session 13 (Volume 5) comprises of:

Reading 46   Market Organization and Structure

Reading 47   Security Market Indices

Reading 48   Market Efficiency

Recommended study time is 11 hours of work.

 Exam focus

This section represents approximately 10% of the exam. Asset classes in total (Equity, Fixed Income, Derivatives and Alternative Investments) represent 30%. It is likely that you will get more equity questions in one of the exams, probably the afternoon and less in the other but overall there will be about 24 questions over the course of the two exams.

There will be some factual questions for which it is simply a question of trying to remember the facts but a greater emphasis will be on conceptual questions regarding the valuation of equities, the characteristics, company analysis and the characteristics of markets as a whole.

Some of the basic quantitative applications are applied to equity valuations but any calculations you are asked to make will not be complex.

 Pre-requisites

Basic quantitative applications (study session 2) should have been studied.

Key areas

- Short positions and leverage positions
- Margining

This section is largely factual and otherwise there are not any areas which are clearly of more importance than others.

Content review – CFA curriculum

2 hours

Most of this reading can be read through in a brief fashion as it provides an introduction to the equity markets. Bear in mind that factual questions can be pulled from any part of this reading.

Section 5 (pages 38-44) on margin, short and levered positions is important to read carefully. Look at examples 19 (page 42) and 20 (page 43).

Section 6 (pages 44-50) on orders and Section 9 (page 58-60) on well-functioning financial systems are also potentially more examinable.

The summary on pages 63-66 covers all the main aspects of the reading and if you are short of time, as well as section 5, you should read this.

Question practice

2 hours

- Attempt all 37 questions at the back of the reading starting on page 67.
- In addition, all questions in the BPP Question Bank should be attempted prior to the exam.

Key areas

- Index calculations and returns

- Index weighting

Content review – CFA curriculum

2 hours

The key sections are at the beginning of this reading.

Section 2 Index Definition and Calculations of Value and Returns (pages 80-84)

Read carefully through this section. Do not be put off by the formulas in section 2.1. You will not have to remember the formulas in a specific format but will need to know how to perform the calculations.

Section 3 Index Construction and Management (pages 84-95)

Read this section fully. The exhibits provide practical examples of the concepts in the text. It is important to understand the advantages / disadvantages of each approach to index construction as well as the methodologies.

Sections 4 – 7 (pages 95-106)

These sections are of lower importance and be read through quickly.

At the end of Section 7 there is a table of worldwide representative indices on pages 105-6. It is worth looking at the first few index descriptions as it is possible you might get a question on a characteristic of a major index.

The summary on page 107 is a useful revision guide.

Question practice

2 hours

- Attempt all 34 questions at the back of this reading starting on page 108.

- In addition, all questions in the BPP Question Bank should be attempted prior to the exam.

STUDY SESSION 13 – READING 48

Market Efficiency (page 119)   **3 hours**

Key areas

- Concept of market efficiency
- Forms of market efficiency (most key)
- Anomalies

Content review – CFA curriculum

1 hour

This is a relatively short but important section which may be examined in more than one question.

Section 2 The Concept of Market Efficiency (pages 121-128)

It is important to understand what us meant by efficiency. This section in general can then be read through reasonably quickly. Work through example 3 (page 123) to ensure you understand what the difference between market value and intrinsic value.

Section 3 Forms of Market Efficiency (pages 128-133)

Read this section carefully. You need to understand the different forms of efficiency and section 3.4 (pages 132-133), the implications of efficient markets hypothesis, is regularly examined.

Sections 4 – 5 (pages 133-143)

These sections are easy reading. It is important you understand what market anomalies exist and why that may be the case. This will also further reinforce your understanding of the efficient markets hypothesis (EMH).

The summary on pages 143-144 is a useful revision guide.

Question practice

2 hours

- Attempt all 26 questions at the back of this reading starting on page 146.
- In addition, all questions in the BPP Question Bank should be attempted prior to the exam.

STUDY GUIDANCE

Equity: Equity Analysis and Valuation

This guidance aims to identify the topics that we consider to be of premium importance for your exam preparation.

Study session 14 (Volume 5) comprises of:

Reading 49   Overview of Equity Securities

Reading 50   Introduction to Industry and Company Analysis

Reading 51   Equity Valuation: Concepts and Basic Tools

Recommended study time is 11 hours of work. Please allow an additional 2 hours to complete Progress Test 7 on Equity Investments.

 ## Exam focus

This section represents approximately 10% of the exam. Asset classes in total (Equity, Fixed Income, Derivatives and Alternative Investments) represent 30%. It is likely that you will get more equity questions in one of the exams, probably the afternoon and less the other but overall there will be about 24 questions over the course of the two exams.

There will be some factual questions for which it is simply a question of trying to remember the facts but a greater emphasis will be on conceptual questions regarding the valuation of equities, the characteristics, company analysis and the characteristics of markets as a whole.

Some of the basic quantitative applications are applied to equity valuations but any calculations you are asked to make will not be complex.

 ## Pre-requisites

Basic quantitative applications (study session 2) should have been studied.

Study session 13 should also have been completed.

Key areas

- This section is either factual or where conceptual, it is covered in other readings

- Equity securities and company value

Content review – CFA curriculum

The reading should be read through in order for you to learn the basic terminologies. You need to know the different sort of investments and what is meant by a number of terms but it is not necessary to go into detail.

Sections 6 and 7 (pages 173-182) are worth reading more carefully concerning risk and company values but the concepts will be covered again in Reading 50.

The summary on pages 182-3 covers the important points and terms you need to know.

1 hour

Question practice

- Attempt all 24 practice problems at the back of this reading starting on page 184.

- In addition, all questions in the BPP Question Bank should be attempted prior to the exam.

2 hours

Key areas

- Industry classifications
- Describing and analysing an industry

Content review – CFA curriculum

Some sections are more key than others.

Section 2 Uses of Industry Analysis (page 192)

Read through quickly, should be self-evident.

Section 3 Approaches to Identifying Different Companies (pages 193-195)

This section is easy reading and should be gone through quickly.

Section 4 Industry Classification Systems (pages 196-206)

Read the description of representative sectors, this covers all the main classifications and see if you can do example 2 (page 198).

Read the sections regarding governmental classifications and read carefully sections 4.3 (page 201) and 4.4 (page 202) regarding weaknesses and peer groups. The CFAI often like to examine your core knowledge by testing your understanding of limitations, weaknesses and advantages / disadvantages of various methodologies.

Section 5 Describing and Analysing an Industry (pages 206-232)

This is the most important section in this reading.

2 hours

Read carefully through the sections. Exhibit 2 (page 208) is a good pictorial summary of industry analysis framework. You should try to learn the 5 Porter determinants of competition on page 210 and read the subsequent detail that follows.

Exhibit 6 on page 219 covers the industry life-cycle model and this is an important subject. You should understand what is meant by the terms used in this context by reading through the detail supporting this exhibit.

You do not need to read through exhibit 7 in detail but it is worth attempting example 8 on page 226.

Section 5.2 (page 226) on external influences is of less importance and it is not necessary to go through the examples.

Section 6 Company Analysis (page 232-237)

This section is of low importance and has been partially covered elsewhere.

The summary for this section on pages 237-240 is quite detailed and is a useful revision guide both now and close to the exam.

Question practice

- Attempt all 31 practice problems at the end of this reading starting on page 241.

- In addition, all questions in the BPP Question Bank should be attempted prior to the exam.

2 hours

STUDY SESSION 14 – READING 51

Equity Valuation: Concepts and Basic Tools (page 247)

4 hours

Very high

Key areas

This section is far more conceptual and historically has been examined quite extensively.

- Dividend discount model
- Preferred stock valuation
- Gordon growth model
- General principals of valuation

Content review – CFA curriculum

Section 2 Estimated Value and Market Price (pages 248-250)

Read through and work through example 1 on page 249.

Section 3 Major Categories of Equity Valuation Models (pages 250-252)

This section is a good introduction for the concepts that follow.

Section 4 Present Value Models: Dividend Discount Model (pages 252-266)

This section is key to understand. It follows concepts introduced in the quantitative applications, (Study Session 2). Do not be put off by the formulas; you do not have to work through all of them. The important formula in the first section is number 3 (page 253). Just focus on this formula then work through example 3 (page 253). You should also work through example 4 (page 254) to cement your understanding.

Section 4.1 Preferred Stock Valuation (page 255)

This follows on from the previous section as you should see from formulas 6 (page 256) and 7 (page 256). Work through example 5 on page 256.

Section 4.2 Gordon's Growth Model (page 258)

2 hours

The concepts underlying this were also introduced in the quantitative applications (Study Session 2). Formulas 9 (page 258) and 10 (page 259) are crucial to remember and you must learn these. Example 6 on page 259 is long winded but will help you re-enforce the concepts and how to use the formulas.

It is important to know the assumptions underlying the model to be able to identify disadvantages and why alternative methods of valuation are sought.

Look at example 7 on page 262 to learn how to apply the model when there are no current dividends. You should recognise the technique from the methods learnt to discount delayed cash flows in the quantitative section, Reading 5.

Section 4.3 Multistage DD Models (page 262)

This section is less important and can be read through quickly.

Section 5 Multiplier Models (page 267)

Some of this section is very important in particular section 5.1 (pages 268-271). You need to understand what the different multiples mean:

- P/E
- P/B
- P/S
- P/CF

Also understand the advantages / disadvantages; you are as likely to be asked to explain a disadvantage as asked to make a calculation of a multiplier.

Section 5.1 Relationships among Price Multiples, Present Value Models, and Fundamentals (page 268)

Formula 14 (page 268) is a key formula you must learn. It is worth working through examples 10 (page 268) and 11 (page 269).

Section 5.2 – Section 6 The Method of Comparables (pages 271-282)

These sections are of lower priority and can be read through briefly without working through the examples.

Question practice

- Attempt all 36 practice problems at the back of this reading starting on page 285.

- In addition, all questions in the BPP Question Bank should be attempted prior to the exam.

2 hours

BPP
LEARNING MEDIA

CHECKPOINT – END OF STUDY SESSIONS 13 AND 14

You are now able to attempt **Progress Test 7 on Equity Investments**.

2 hours

NOTES

Progress Test 7 – Equity Investments

Questions

1. Which of the following is *least accurate* when describing private equity securities?

    A. They are issued to institutional investors via a private placement.

    B. Enable holders to receive a dividend and may include a share of profits above a pre-specified amount.

    C. They do not trade in secondary equity markets.

2. A firm is expected to pay dividends per share of $0.50 in one year's time. Dividends are then expected to grow by 8% for the next two years, and thereafter by 4% each year. The market value of the shares, if the rate of return required by shareholders is 9%, is *closest* to:

    A. $10.00.

    B. $10.70.

    C. $11.80.

3. From an investor's point of view, which of the following equity securities is the *most* risky?

    A. Preference shares.

    B. Common shares.

    C. Putable common shares.

4. Which of the following would contradict the semi-strong form of the efficient market hypothesis?

    A. High beta stocks earning high returns.

    B. Directors of a company making supernormal profits on share dealing.

    C. A company experiencing excess positive returns after an earnings surprise.

5. Which of the following is *least accurate* when describing Global Depository Receipts?

    A. GDRs are not subject to foreign ownership restriction rules imposed by the issuing company's home country.

    B. GDRs are US$ denominated and trade like common shares on U.S. exchanges.

    C. GDRs can be sponsored or unsponsored.

6. Company XYZ Inc's primary source of revenue comes from the manufacturing of luxury leather goods. Based on this information, which of the following representative sectors within the Global Industry Classification Standards (GICS) is *most appropriate* for XYZ Inc?

    A. Consumer Discretionary.

    B. Consumer Staples.

    C. Basic Materials and Processing.

7.   Which of the following is *least* likely to be a characteristic of a well-functioning securities market?

   A. Timely information on the volume of shares traded.

   B. Low brokerage costs.

   C. Prices that react steadily and slowly to new information.

8.   Which of the following *most* likely to be a characteristic of a continuous market?

   A. Used when there is an overnight build up of buy or sell orders.

   B. Stocks are priced by auction or dealers.

   C. Uses a single price that will satisfy most of the orders at any one time.

9.   An increase in which of the following variables is *most likely* to increase the value of a company?

   A. Long term sustainable growth rate.

   B. Investors required return.

   C. Dividend yield.

10. An analyst has obtained the following data on a stock market series.

Expected dividend payout ratio	25%
Shareholders' required return	12%
Return on equity	15%
Risk-free rate of return	4%

   The expected price earnings ratio of the stock market series is *closest to*:

   A. 7 times.

   B. 8 times.

   C. 33 times.

11. Which of the following is *least likely* to be an attribute to the shakeout of an industry life cycle?

   A. Slow growth.

   B. Excess industry capacity exists.

   C. Focus on cost cutting sees rise in profits.

12. If all other factors remain unchanged, which of the following events would *most likely* reduce a firm's price-to-earnings (P/E) ratio?

   A. Investors become less risk averse.

   B. The dividend payout ratio increases.

   C. The yield on Treasury bills increases.

13. A stock has a required return of 15 percent, a constant growth rate of 10 percent, and a dividend payout ratio of 45 percent. The stock's price-to-earnings (P/E) ratio is *most likely* to be:

    A. 3.0.

    B. 4.5.

    C. 9.0.

14. Which of the following is *least* likely to be a limitation to achieve fully efficient markets?

    A. Pricing anomalies.

    B. Cost of trading.

    C. Cost of information.

15. Which of the following industry is *most affected* by demographic influences?

    A. Pharmaceuticals.

    B. Oil services.

    C. Confections and Candy.

16. Common stock pays an annual dividend per share of $3.17. The risk premium for this stock is 3% and the risk-free rate is 7%. Next year's dividend is expected to be $3.58 and thereafter to remain at this level. The share price according to the dividend discount model is *closest to*:

    A. $31.70.

    B. $35.80.

    C. $45.30.

17. Which of the following is *least likely* to be considered in a company analysis?

    A. Review of corporate governance procedures.

    B. Analysis of the demand for the company's products.

    C. Discussions with key management.

18. An investor buys a stock on margin. The initial margin is 60% and the maintenance margin is 25%. The price of the stock is $10. At what price would he be asked to make a margin call?

    A. $6.00.

    B. $5.33.

    C. $3.50.

19. If an investor believes that the weak form of the efficient market hypothesis holds, then the investor is *least likely* to use:

    A. Index tracking.

    B. Technical analysis.

    C. Fundamental analysis.

20. A stock has a beta of 1.2. It has just paid a dividend of $12.50 and is expected to generate dividends of $14.00 in one year's time, $15.40 in two years' time and $16.50 in three years' time. Thereafter, the dividends are expected to grow at a rate of 4% each year. If the return expected from the market portfolio is 9% and the risk-free rate of return is 3.5%, the estimated value of the stock is *closest to*:

   A. $229.

   B. $242.

   C. $249.

21. Which of the following *most* likely to be true of the Nikkei – stock average Index?

	WEIGHTING	NO. OF STOCKS
A.	Value	225
B.	Value	30
C.	Price	225

22. A company that has a stock split will cause a downward bias in which type of weighted index?

   A. Price weighted.

   B. Value weighted.

   C. Unweighted.

23. Which of the following is *most likely* to be a characteristic of an industry with high barriers to entry?

   A. High level of concentration.

   B. High price competition.

   C. Low industry stability.

24. An analyst gathers the following information for a price-weighted index comprised of securities X, Y and Z:

Security	Beginning of period price/£	End of period price/£	Total dividends/£
X	17	19	1/50
Y	22	15	2.00
Z	10	11	0.50

The price return of the index is:

   A. -6.3%.

   B. -7.5%.

   C. -8.2%.

25. A company, which has just paid its annual dividend, has a payout ratio of 50%, an expected dividend growth rate of 2% p.a. compound and a required return on equity of 12% p.a. What is the company's forward P/E ratio?

    A. 5.1.

    B. 5.0.

    C. 4.3.

26. Which of the following is least likely to be a feature of commodity indices?

    A. Returns of commodity indices that include the same commodities can differ.

    B. A commodity index return matches the return based on changes in the prices of the underlying commodities.

    C. Commodity indices consist of futures contracts on one or more commodities.

27. ABC Company has 8% nonconvertible preferred stock with a par value of $100. You are considering purchasing the ABC preferred stock or, alternatively, buying a corporate bond yielding 10.5%. If investors require a 12% rate of return, how much should be paid for the preferred stock?

    A. $66.67.

    B. $76.19.

    C. $83.33.

28. Which of the following factors is *least likely* to cause a difference between the P/E ratio of two stocks?

    A. The expected payout ratio.

    B. The required rate of return.

    C. The expected real growth rate of the economy.

29. Which of the following is true of the weak form of the efficient market hypothesis?

    A. It implies that market price information cannot be used to identify future price movements.

    B. It implies that stock prices react to information when it becomes publicly available.

    C. It implies that insiders cannot make a profit from their trading.

30. Which of the following is *least likely* to occur when markets are considered strong form efficient?

    A. Investors will consider market prices to equal intrinsic value.

    B. A passive investment strategy is preferred.

    C. All market participants behave rationally.

Progress Test 7 – Equity Investments

1. **B**   This is a description of a participating preference share, not private equity

   See LOS 49c

2. **B**   Market value = $\dfrac{0.5}{1.09} + \dfrac{0.5 \times 1.08}{1.09^2} + \dfrac{0.5 \times 1.08^2}{1.09^3} + \dfrac{0.5 \times 1.08^2 \times 1.04}{0.09 - 0.04} \times \dfrac{1}{1.09^3}$

                    $= 0.459 + 0.455 + 0.450 + 9.367 = \$10.73$

   Note that we discount the growing perpetuity by 3 years even though the fist payment is at time 4. This is because the first payment in a perpetuity is always one period after the point we value it at

   You can also perform this calculation viewing it as growing perpetuity starting at time 2, as growth is 4% from that point onwards. This would give you the same final answer

   See LOS 51e

3. **B**   Preference shares rank above common shares with respect to dividends, so therefore have less risk. Putable common shares allow the investor to exercise a put option to sell the shares if prices fall below certain predetermined price – this gives downside protection and therefore less risk to the investor than a common share

   See LOS 49e

4. **C**   This indicates that the positive information contained in the earnings surprise is not immediately reflected in the stock price

   See LOS 48d

5. **B**   GDRs trade outside of the U.S. ADRs trade on U.S markets

   See LOS 49d

6. **A**   Consumer discretionary is for companies that sell consumer-related products whose demand trends to exhibit a high degree of economic sensitivity, e.g. luxury items such as leather goods

   See LOS 50b

7. **C**   Prices need to adjust rapidly to new information so that prevailing market prices reveal all the available information

   See LOS 46k

8. **B**   The other answers are characteristics of a call market

   See LOS 46i

9. **A** The value of a share is very sensitive to the long run growth rate, therefore this will have the biggest positive impact. An increase in the required return will reduce the discounted dividend value. The dividend yield is not directly part of the pricing formula

    See LOS 51c

10. **C** g = retention rate × ROE

    = (1 − Payout ratio) × ROE

    = 0.75 × 0.15 = 0.1125

    P/E ratio = $\dfrac{d_1}{e_1} \times \dfrac{1}{r_e - g}$ = Payout ratio × $\dfrac{1}{r_e - g}$

    = 0.25 × $\dfrac{1}{0.12 - 0.1125}$ = 33

    See LOS 51h

11. **C** Companies do focus on cost cutting but prices are reduced to boost demand, hence reducing profitability

    See LOS 50g

12. **C** Based on $\dfrac{P}{E} = \dfrac{d_1}{e_1} \times \dfrac{1}{r_e - g}$

    where $\dfrac{d_1}{e_1}$ is the payout ratio

    An increase in yield on Treasury bills will increase r_e, the required rate of return

    See LOS 51h

13. **C** P/E = Dividend payout ratio × $\dfrac{1}{r_e - g}$

    = 0.45 × $\dfrac{1}{0.15 - 0.10}$

    = 9.0

    See LOS 51h

14. **A** Pricing anomolies are mispricings that are known and persistent. They do not prevent an efficient market, B and C are limitations as is limits of arbitrage

    See LOS 48c

15. **A** Populations of developed markets are ageing which can increase demand in the pharmaceutical industry

    See LOS 50j

16. **B** Share price = $\dfrac{3.58}{0.03 + 0.07}$ = \$35.80

    See LOS 51e

17. **C** Company analysis does not include discussions with management. It is a paper exercise, using all published information

See LOS 50k

18. **B** The margin call occurs at $10 \times \dfrac{(1-0.6)}{(1-0.25)}$

The broker lends 40% initially, i.e. $4. If the price drops to $5.33, the investor's equity balance is $1.33, so the investor's equity has dropped to 25% of the investment and a margin call will be required

See LOS 46f

19. **B** Since the weak form EMH states that all historic market information has already been incorporated into the current stock price

See LOS 48e

20. **C** Required rate of return = 3.5 + 1.2 (9 – 3.5) = 10.1%

$$\text{Value} \;=\; \frac{14}{1.101}+\frac{15.4}{1.101^2}+\frac{16.5}{1.101^3}+\frac{16.5\times1.04}{0.101-0.04}\times\frac{1}{1.101^3}$$

$$= 12.72 + 12.70 + 12.36 + 210.78$$

$$= 248.56$$

See LOS 51e

21. **C** Dow Jones indexes are price weighted

See LOS 47k

22. **A** When a company has a stock split their price per share falls and therefore so does their weighting in the index. High growth stocks are the ones that tend to have stock splits

See LOS 47c

23. **A** High barriers to entry such as brand names or high R&D expense, usually mean a small number of companies control the bulk of the market. Price competition is usually low because it is determined by factors other than competition, such as brand familiarity. Industry stability tends to be high because the market is made up of large dominant players rather than smaller players that come and go

See LOS 50h

24. **C** Percentage change in price = 45 – 49/49 = -8.16%

See LOS 47e

25. **B** $P/E = \dfrac{0.5}{0.12-0.02} = 5$

See LOS 51h

26. **B** Because the index consists of futures on commodities, the returns of the index and the returns of underlying commodities are different. The index return is impacted by the roll yield of the futures

   See LOS 47j

27. **A** The value of a preferred stock is equal to the dividend amount divided by the required rate of return

   $$\frac{\$8.00}{12\%} = \$66.67$$

   The calculation is a perpetuity because preferred stock has no maturity

   See LOS 51d

28. **C** P/E ratio = $\dfrac{d_1}{e_1} \times \dfrac{1}{r_e - g}$

   The expected payout ratio affects the P/E (the higher the payout ratio, the higher the P/E). The required rate of return affects the P/E ratio (the higher the required rate of return, the lower the P/E ratio). A change in the growth rate of the economy will impact both stocks, therefore C is the most appropriate answer

   See LOS 51h

29. **A** The weak form of the EMH states that all market price information has already been incorporated into the current stock price

   See LOS 48d

30. **C** A market can still be considered efficient even if market participants exhibit irrational behaviour such as herding

   See LOS 48d

STUDY GUIDANCE

Fixed Income: Basic Concepts

This guidance aims to identify the topics that we consider to be of premium importance for your exam preparation.

Study session 15 (Volume 5) comprises of:

Reading 52   Fixed-income Securities: Defining Elements

Reading 53   Fixed-income Markets: Issuance, Trading, and Funding

Reading 54   Introduction to Fixed-income Valuation

Recommended study time is 6.5 hours of work.

 Exam focus

This section represents approximately 12% of the exam. Assets in total (Equity, Fixed Income, Derivatives and Alternative Investments) represent 30%. It is likely that you will get more fixed income questions in one of the exams, probably the morning and less the other, but overall there will be about 28 questions over the course of the two exams.

There will be some factual questions for which it is simply a question of trying to remember the facts but also conceptual questions as well.

For interest only, up until last year, these readings were written by Frank J. Fabozzi. He is arguably the most famous author in the world for writing about bonds and fixed income and has published a lot of books. However, the entire Fixed Income sections have been rewritten for 2014 and a number of additional LOS have been added and much of the material has been updated. It is therefore important to focus on these new areas of the syllabus which have not been tested previously.

 Pre-requisites

Basic quantitative applications (study session 2) should have been studied. You need to be familiar with the discounted cash flow functions of your Texas calculator.

You may find that it makes sense to leave Readings 53 and 54 until after the other readings in these two study sessions (15 and 16) on fixed income.

STUDY SESSION 15 – READING 52

Fixed-income Securities: Defining Elements (page 299)   **2 hours**

Key areas

- This is a key introductory chapter and necessary to understand the forthcoming readings, particularly for those not familiar with fixed income products or bond markets

Content review – CFA curriculum

The whole of this reading should be read (pages 299-340). It is largely factual rather than conceptual. The summary section is long reflecting the amount of facts contained in this section and if you feel comfortable with what you have learnt or are familiar with bonds, then you can miss out the summary.   **1 hour**

You may find the BPP Passcards an efficient way to study this section.

Question practice

- Attempt all questions (page 341) as these are all of the style that you can expect to see in the real exam.   **1 hour**

- In addition, all questions in the BPP Question Bank should be attempted prior to the exam.

Key areas

- Most of this section is important background reading especially for those new to fixed income and is necessary preparation for later readings

Content review – CFA curriculum

Large parts of this reading are background information/descriptive but need to be read in order for you to have a full understanding of the concepts which follow in the later readings.

Read through the section carefully and attempt the examples as you work through the chapter. As all are set out as you would expect to see in the exam and are good practice. The summary is worth reading on pages 388-9.

1.5 hours

Question practice

- Attempt all the questions starting on page 390.

- In addition, all questions in the BPP Question Bank should be attempted prior to the exam.

1 hour

Key areas

- There are a number of calculation areas in this chapter, such as flat price, accrued interest and full price as well as the various yield measures. The chapter also considers the differences between the spot and forward curve and how to calculate either spot or forward rates given a certain starting point. These areas are highly examinable and lend themselves well to the multiple choice style questions

Content review – CFA curriculum

You should read through this chapter completely and work through the examples as appropriate.

You will need to learn the basis for the calculations and ensure you are comfortable with this both in the calculation methodology and the general principles. Often you will find questions which test calculation methodology rather than asking you to perform the actual calculation.

Section 2 (page 398)

This section covers material that you have met before with the time value of money. Try example 1 on page 400 and example 2 on page 402 to recap your knowledge in this area.

Section 2.3 (page 403)

This section provides a good description of bond price and characteristics which is worth reading.

Section 2.4 (page 407)

This is an important area covering pricing bonds with spot rates and needs to be read.

1.5 hours

Section 3 (page 409)

Prices and Yields: conventions for quotes and valuations: can be read through quickly, but do look at examples 5 on page 411 and 6 on page 415 for exam-style questions. Example 8 on page 418 could be worked through if you have time, but is above that which would be expected in the exam. Section 3.4, yield measures for floating rate notes, is key and should be worked through and examples 9 (page 423) and 10 (page 427) are good to test your learning.

Sections 4 and 5: the maturity structure of interest rates, and Yield Spreads, are both key areas and you should read through them and work through the examples. Equation 15 on page 440 is important to remember and often features in the exam.

The summary is a useful recap but you will need to work through the chapter for a fuller understanding.

Question practice

- Attempt all 44 practice questions starting on page 444 for examples of what you may see in the exam.

30 minutes

- In addition, all questions in the BPP Question Bank should be attempted prior to the real exam.

STUDY GUIDANCE

Fixed Income: Analysis of Risk

This guidance aims to identify the topics that we consider to be of premium importance for your exam preparation.

Study session 16 (Volume 5) comprises of:

Reading 55   Understanding Fixed-income Risk and Return

Reading 56   Fundamentals of Credit Analysis

Recommended study time is 14 hours of work. An additional 2 hours should be added to complete Progress Test 8 on Fixed Income Instruments.

 ## Exam focus

This section represents approximately 12% of the exam. Assets in total (Equity, Fixed Income, Derivatives and Alternative Investments) represent 30%. It is likely that you will get more fixed income questions in one of the exams, probably the morning and less the other, but overall there will be about 28 questions over the course of the two exams.

There will be some factual questions for which it is simply a question of trying to remember the facts but also conceptual questions as well.

 ## Pre-requisites

Basic quantitative applications (study session 2) should have been studied. You need to be familiar with the discounted cash flow functions of your Texas calculator.

You should have completed Readings 52 and 55 in study session 15 before attempting this study session.

Key areas

The duration measures are important, as are the valuation of bonds with embedded options.

This is followed up with calculation of an overall portfolio duration and the impact of convexity. The last section is somewhat easier to read with descriptions of te types of risk that may affect a bond portfolio.

Content review – CFA curriculum

Section 2 Sources of Return (page 470)

Read through the whole section and work through the examples (the early ones are more indicative of exam standard. Examples 4, 5 and 6 are over complicated but if you understand them you will certainly be able to cope with the questions in the exam on this topic).

Section 3 Interest Rate Risk on Fixed Rate Bonds (page 477)

You need to learn the different methods for calculating duration and learn the equations. Example 9 is worth working through on page 486. Example 10 on page 490, whilst over complicated as an exam style question, is well worth working through as it tests in detail all the knowledge built up in the previous section.

Section 3.4 Duration of a Bond Portfolio (page 494)

Read this section and work through example 11 on page 495.

Section 3.5 Money Duration of a Bond and Price Value of a Basis Point (page 496)

Another section that must be read. It is important to learn equation 12 on page 497 to then work through example 12 on the same page.

5 hours

Section 3.6 Bond Convexity (page 498)

This has never been covered in such depth before, and it would be well worth looking over and understanding Exhibit 10 on page 498 and learning and understanding equations 13, 14 and 15 on page 499.

Section 4 Interest Rate Risk and the Investment Horizon (page 506)

This section should be read through, with attention paid to Exhibit 13 on page 511 for a good graphical depiction of the main points.

Section 5 Credit and Liquidity Risk (page 513)

A very short section and less important than the preceding sections but it is worth reading through quickly.

The summary on page 514 is fairly lengthy and comprehensive and is worth an overview.

Question practice

- Attempt all the practice problems starting on page 518.

- In addition, all questions in the BPP Question Bank should be attempted prior to the exam.

2 hours

Key areas

This chapter is more about theory than calculation and involves a lot of reading and remembering, although having said that, much of it is less examinable than previous chapters and is more to aid the background understanding of the topic area.

Content review – CFA curriculum

Sections 2, 3, and 4 should be read through, with focus paid to Exhibit 1 on debt seniority (page 533) and Exhibit 4, long term ratings matrix (page 539) and try to remember the distinction between investment grade and non-investment grade ratings. (If it starts with a C, or if it starts with a B and has two or less letters, it is non investment grade.)

Section 5 Traditional Credit Analysis: Corporate Debt Securities (page 547)

Read through, focussing on section 5.2 (page 548) and example 5 (page 551). The rest of the reading is similar to material covered previously in Financial Reporting and is fairly long winded. It also contains some fairly lengthy examples which do not add much value.

Section 6 Credit Risk v Return (page 566)

5 hours

Read through this section, paying particular attention to the section on yield spreads.

Section 7 Special Considerations of High Yield, Sovereign, and Municipal Credit Analysis (page 576)

Again, worth reading through quickly, although there appears to be less examinable material in this section.

Section 8 Conclusion and Summary (page 589)

The conclusion and summary is fairly comprehensive and should be read through to consolidate learning after you have worked through the chapter, or as part of a revision strategy rather than referring back to the rather lengthy wording in the main chapter.

Question practice

- Attempt all the practice problems starting on page 594.

2 hours

- In addition, all questions in the BPP Question Bank should be attempted prior to the exam.

CHECKPOINT – END OF STUDY SESSIONS 15 AND 16

You are now able to attempt **Progress Test 8 on Fixed-income Investments**.

2 hours

Progress Test 8 – Fixed-income Investments

Questions

1. An annual coupon bond is priced at 114, has a yield of 8% and has a modified duration of 3.4. If yields rise by 50 basis points what will be *closest to* the new price of the bond?

   A. 112.06.

   B. 112.16.

   C. 115.84.

2. Which of the following bonds will be *most likely* to give the greatest reinvestment risk, given the same yield to maturity for all the bonds?

   A. 10-year 5% coupon.

   B. 10-year 2% coupon.

   C. 20-year zero coupon.

3. Investors who believe interest rates will fall would be most likely to invest in:

   A. Fixed rate bonds.

   B. Inverse floaters.

   C. Floating rate notes.

4. Which of the following *best describes* negative convexity?

   A. The tendency of the callable bond price to rise less quickly than that of an equivalent straight bond when interest rates fall.

   B. The fact that the actual price change of a bond is always greater than that predicted by modified duration.

   C. The fact that there is an inverse relationship between bond price changes and yield changes.

5. Which of the following spread measures would be *most useful* when analysing a mortgage-backed security (MBS)?

   A. Cash flow yield spread.

   B. Nominal spread.

   C. Option-adjusted spread.

6. Which of the following statements about duration is incorrect?

   A. A bond's modified duration cannot be larger than its Macauley duration.

   B. Curve duration measures the sensitivity of the market value of a financial asset with respect to a benchmark yield curve.

   C. Effective duration is a measure of yield duration.

7. A two-year 8% bond paying interest semi-annually is bought on a yield of 9%. It is sold six months later on a yield of 10%. Which of the following is *closest to* the holding period return?

   A. −0.9%.

   B. 1.0%.

   C. 3.1%.

8. An analyst determines that an 8% option-free bond would experience a 3% change in price if market interest rates were to increase by 50 bps. If market rates were to fall by 50 bps, the bond's price will *most likely*:

   A. Increase by less that 3%.

   B. Decrease by less than 3%.

   C. Increase by more than 3%.

9. Which of the following is *least likely* to be a limitation of the current yield?

   A. It assumes that the coupons can be reinvested at the current yield until maturity.

   B. It only considers the coupon flows.

   C. It ignores the timing of cash flows.

10. The embedded option that is *most likely* to be a benefit to a holder of debt securities is the:

    A. Call provision in a callable bond.

    B. Cap on a floater.

    C. Put provision in a putable bond.

11. An investment in a coupon bond will provide the investor with a return equal to the bond's yield to maturity at the time of purchase if:

    A. The bond is called for redemption at a price that exceeds its par value.

    B. The bond contains a put option that is favorable to the investor.

    C. The reinvestment rate is the same as the bond's yield to maturity.

12. Bond price volatility for an option-free bond normally is *most likely* to be:

    A. Lower for higher coupons.

    B. Lower for longer duration.

    C. Greater for shorter maturities.

13. Which of the following statements about the term structure of interest rates is *most accurate*?

   A. The expectations hypothesis contends that the long-term rate is equal to the anticipated short-term rate.

   B. The liquidity preference theory indicates that, all else being equal, longer maturities will have lower yields.

   C. The segmented market theory contends that borrowers and lenders prefer particular segments of the yield curve.

14. A treasury bill with 80 days from settlement to maturity is selling for $0.982 per $1 par. What is *closest to* the yield on a discount rate basis?

   A. 1.8%.

   B. 8.1%.

   C. 8.6%.

15. Relative to an otherwise similar option free bond, a

   A. callable bond will trade at a lower price.

   B. putable bond will trade at a lower price.

   C. convertible bond will trade at a lower price.

16. When a company's credit spread increases as a result of an increase in perception that there is a risk of default, this is *most likely* referred to as:

   A. Default risk.

   B. Downgrade risk.

   C. Credit spread risk.

17. Which of the following is a source of wholesale funding for banks?

   A. Interbank funds.

   B. Money market accounts.

   C. Checking accounts.

18. Which of the following is the best measure of volatility to use for a callable bond?

   A. Effective convexity.

   B. Effective duration.

   C. Modified duration.

19. Using the following information, what is the one-year implied forward rate one year from now? Assume effective annual rates.

Year	Spot Rate
1	5.00%
2	6.50%
3	4.75%

 A. 4.750%.

 B. 6.500%.

 C. 8.021%.

20. In the event of a default, the recovery rate of which of the following bonds would *most likely* be the lowest?

 A. Junior subordinate debt.

 B. Senior unsecured debt.

 C. First mortgage debt.

21. The yield to maturity on a four-year 6% annual pay coupon bond, priced at $950, is *closest to*:

 A. 6.83%.

 B. 7.36%.

 C. 7.49%.

22. Which of the following is *least likely* to be a weakness of the yield to maturity calculation for a bond?

 A. It ignores any capital gain on maturity.

 B. It assumes the bond is held to maturity.

 C. It assumes a constant interest rate to maturity.

23. Which of the following is the *most likely* reason for an inverted yield curve?

 A. Liquidity factors.

 B. Investors buying long-dated bonds due to interest rate expectations.

 C. Risk factors.

24. When interest rates are very low, which of the following is *most accurate* in respect of effective duration compared to modified duration for a callable and putable bond?

 Effective duration will be .... than/to modified duration

	CALLABLE BOND	PUTABLE BOND
A.	Lower	Lower
B.	Lower	Similar
C.	Similar	Lower

25. A bond has a yield to maturity of 7% and a modified duration of 7. If the yield decreases by 2%, the approximate percentage price change predicted using the duration concept is *closest to*:

    A. 3.5% increase.

    B. 7.0% decrease.

    C. 14.0% increase.

26. Which of the following is the *most accurate* description of the difference between modified convexity and effective convexity?

    A. Modified convexity is expressed in absolute terms whereas effective convexity is a relative measure.

    B. Modified convexity gives an approximate level of convexity whereas effective convexity is completely accurate.

    C. Modified convexity is not suitable for bonds with embedded options whereas effective convexity is.

27. An investor has a portfolio containing three bonds, with market values of $1m, $2m and $5m. Their durations are 3.5, 4 and 6 respectively. What is *closest to* the total portfolio duration?

    A. 4.5.

    B. 5.2.

    C. 13.5.

28. Which of the following risks is *least appropriate* in interpreting the z-spread of a bond?

    A. Credit.

    B. Liquidity.

    C. Volatility.

29. For an upward sloping yield curve, which is *most likely* to be correct? The z-spread:

    A. Increases with maturity.

    B. Is constant across all maturities.

    C. Is greater than the option adjusted (OAS).

30. For a bond with an embedded put, its option cost will be:

    A. Negative because z-spread is less than OAS.

    B. Positive because z-spread is less than OAS.

    C. Negative because z-spread is greater than OAS.

31. Which of the following statements about Macauley Duration is incorrect?

    A. A bonds yield to maturity is inversely related to its Macauley Duration.

    B. The Macauley Duration of a zero coupon bond equals its time to maturity.

    C. A bond's Macauley Duration and coupon rate are positively related.

32. You have been given the following information about three bonds that comprise a portfolio. Assume annual coupon payments and no accrued interest on the bonds. Prices are per 100 of par value:

Bond	Maturity	Market value	Price	Modified duration
A	4 years	130,000	90,000	5.92%
B	8 years	100,000	75,000	7.89%
C	16 years	80,000	100,000	10.22%

The bond portfolio's modified duration is closest to:

A. 6.23%.

B. 7.67%.

C. 8.10%.

33. A pension fund manager is seeking to measure the sensitivity of their pension liabilities to market interest rate changes. He determines the present value of the liabilities under three interest rate scenarios: a base rate of 4%, a 200 basis point increase up to 6% and a 200 basis point drop in rates to 2%. The results of the analysis are as follows:

Interest rate assumption	Present value of liabilities
2%	GBP 450.2 million
4%	GBP 342.5 million
6%	GBP 276.7 million

The effective duration of the funds liabilities is closest to:

A. 6.33%.

B. 12.66%.

C. 14.24%.

34. Holding all other factors equal, the most likely effect of high demand and low new issue supply on bond yield spreads is that yield spreads will likely:

A. widen.

B. tighten.

C. not be affected.

Progress Test 8 – Fixed Income Investments

Answers

1. **A**   Price change = $114 \times 0.005 \times (3.4) = -1.94$

    New price = $114 - 1.94 = 112.06$

    See LOS 55h

2. **A**   Longest dated and highest coupon (the zero will have no reinvestment risk)

    See LOS 52e

3. **B**   The coupon on an inverse floater will increase as interest rates fall but this will be favoured. The coupon on the floating rate note will decrease, and the coupon on the fixed rate bond will be unaffected

    See LOS 52a

4. **A**   This is because the rise in the price of the bond is offset by the rise in the value of the issuer's call option. The bond price approaches its price ceiling

    See LOS 55d

5. **C**   The OAS strips out prepayment risk and leaves us with a clean measure of credit and liquidity risk to enable comparison to other bonds

    See LOS 54j

6. **C**   Effective duration is a measure of curve duration not yield duration

    See LOS 55b

7. **C**   Purchase price = $\dfrac{4}{1.045} + \dfrac{4}{1.045^2} + \dfrac{4}{1.045^3} + \dfrac{104}{1.045^4} = 98.21$

    Sale price = $\dfrac{4}{1.05} + \dfrac{4}{1.05^2} + \dfrac{104}{1.05^3} = 97.28$

    Return = $\dfrac{101.28}{98.21} - 1 = 3.1\%$

    Note that the coupon of 4 must also be included in the return calculation

    See LOS 54b

8. **C**   The convex nature of the price-yield relationship will cause prices to fall by more than they would rise given an opposite yield movement of the same magnitude

    See LOS 55h

9. **A**   The current yield ignores any reinvestment income. This would be a limitation of the yield to maturity

    See LOS 54b

10. **C**   Bonds with a call provision enable the issuer to repurchase the bonds at a set price prior to its stated maturity, meaning that the bond price will not rise as much as the price of a comparable straight bond when interest rates fall. The cap on a floater restricts the maximum coupon that will be paid, meaning that the holder will be disadvantaged if the cap is exercised. The put provision effectively establishes a floor to the price of the bond for the investor

      See LOS 54f

11. **C**   The yield to maturity calculation also assumes that the bond is held to maturity

      See LOS 54b

12. **A**   Bond price volatility is inversely related to coupon and directly related to maturity

      See LOS 55d

13. **C**   The expectations hypothesis contends that the shape of the yield curve results from interest rate expectations. The liquidity preference hypothesis contends that the yield curve should be upward sloping since investors are willing to sacrifice some yield to avoid the higher price volatility of long-term maturity bonds

      See LOS 55d

14. **B**   The holding period return is 1.8% and the effective annual return (compounded) is 8.6%. The yield on a discount basis, *d*, is given by:

   $$d = 1 - 0.982 \times \frac{360}{80} = 8.1\%$$

      See LOS 54f

15. **A**   As a call option is beneficial to the issuer, the bond will generally trade at a lower price than a similar option free bond. The put option and the conversion option are beneficial to the bondholder, and would *most likely* add a premium on to the price

      See LOS 52f

16. **C**   The credit spread has increased as a result of the increased risk of default

      LOS 56h

17. **A**   Interbank funds are one of the sources of funds for banks. The other two are incorrect as they are retail deposits not wholesale funds

      See LOS 53f

18. **B**   Effective duration will give the same answer as modified duration for an option-free bond. But when there are option features, modified duration does not model them in, thus gives misleading result

      See LOS 55c

19. **C**   One-year implied forward rate in one year's time $= \dfrac{1.065^2}{1.05} - 1$

      See LOS 54h

20. **A**   Junior subordinated debt generally ranks lowest in seniority in a wind up

       See LOS 56b

21. **C**   Using the following calculator entries we can solve for the yield on an annual pay basis: 4N, 60 PMT, 1000 FV, −950 PV = 7.49%. This is the effective annual rate or annual pay basis

       See LOS 54f

22. **A**   The yield to maturity considers both income and capital gains/losses

       See LOS 54g

23. **B**   If investors expect rates to fall, they will buy long-dated bonds, increasing long-dated bond prices and decreasing long yields

       See LOS 54g

24. **B**   Due to price compression for the callable bond. The putable bond exhibits price truncation at high rates of interest, not at low rates

       See LOS 55c

25. **C**   The duration gives the approximate percentage change for a 1% change in yield

       See LOS 55b

26. **C**   The modified convexity calculation assumes that the cash flows are unaffected by changes in yields

       See LOS 55g

27. **B**   Portfolio duration is a weighted average by market value of the bonds in the portfolio

       See LOS 55e

28. **C**   The z-spread includes credit, liquidity and option risk but not volatility

       See LOS 54i

29. **B**   The z-spread is always constant for any shape of the yield curve. This is a limitation in the model, as in reality there is a term structure to spreads

       See LOS 54i

30. **A**   Option cost = z-spread minus OAS for any bond. For puts, the OAS is higher than the z-spread, so that option cost for a put is negative

       See LOS 54i

31. **C**   A bond's Macauley duration and coupon rate are negatively correlated

       See LOS 55b

32. **B**   The portfolio's modified duration is closest to 7.67% as it is the market value weighted average of the yield durations of the individual bonds in the portfolio

       (5.92 x 130/310) + (7.89 x 130/310) + (10.22 x 80/310)

       See LOS 55b

33. **B** The effective duration is calculated by reference to the formula:

$$\text{Effective duration} = \frac{\left[\left(Pv-\right)-\left(Pv+\right)\right]}{2\times\Delta \text{ curve}\times\left(Pv_0\right)}$$

See LOS 55b

34. **B** Higher demand will tighten yield spreads, and low new supply will tighten them even further, so B is the most appropriate answer

See LOS 56h

STUDY GUIDANCE

Derivatives

This guidance aims to identify the topics that we consider to be of premium importance for your exam preparation.

Study session 17 (Volume 6) comprises of:

Reading 57   Derivative Markets and Instruments

Reading 58   Forward Markets and Contracts

Reading 59   Futures Markets and Contracts

Reading 60   Option Markets and Contracts

Reading 61   Swap Market and Contracts

Reading 62   Risk Management Applications of Option Strategies

Recommended study time is 20.5 hours of work. An additional 2 hours should be added to complete Progress Test 9 on Derivatives.

 ## Exam focus

This section represents approximately 5% of the exam. Assets in total (Equity, Fixed Income, Derivatives and Alternative Investments) represent 30%.

You are not expected to be a derivatives expert and more the focus is on understanding the descriptions of the products and the basics of how they work rather than complex valuations.

Given the small percentage of this section, you should plan your revision accordingly and not allocate more than the necessary time to this area, focusing on the key points only.

 ## Pre-requisites

There are no pre-requisites to this study session.

STUDY SESSION 17 – READING 57

Derivatives Markets and Instruments (page 5)   **3 hours**

Key areas

- General knowledge of forwards, futures, options and swaps
- Understand arbitrage and the principles of derivative pricing

Content review – CFA curriculum

This section can be read through very quickly. For those familiar with derivatives you can just skip   **2 hours**
to the summary section on page 52.

Question practice

                                                                                    1 hour

- Attempt all 15 practice problems at the back of this reading, starting on page 55.
- In addition, all questions in the BPP Question Bank should be attempted prior to the real exam.

Key areas

- Forwards
- FRAs

Content review – CFA curriculum

Section 1 – 1.3 Introduction (pages 61-64)

Read through this section – it should be quick.

Section 2 Global Forwards Markets (pages 64-66)

Non-key this section can be skipped.

2 hours

Section 3 Types of Forward Contracts (pages 66-73)

This is the key section in this reading; make sure you understand how the different sorts of forwards work and in particular how FRAs are priced.

The summary is a good revision guide and begins on page 73.

Question practice

- There are only 3 practice problems at the back of this reading on page 75. You should attempt all of them.

30 minutes

- In addition, all questions in the BPP Question Bank should be attempted prior to the exam.

Key areas

- Characteristics of futures
- Margining

Content review – CFA curriculum

Sections 1 and 2 (pages 77-82)

This is largely background reading and can be read through quickly.

Section 3 The Clearinghouse, Margins and Limits (pages 82-88)

This section is important and you should read through it carefully making sure you understand what is meant by the various terms as well as how to calculate margin requirements. Example 1 on page 86 is a comprehensive example worth going through.

Section 4 Delivery and Cash Settlement (pages 88-90)

Understand the daily settlement process.

Sections 5 and 6 Futures Exchanges and Types of Futures (pages 90-91)

Background reading, you can just gloss over these sections.

4 hours

Section 6.1 Short Term Interest Rate Contracts (pages 93-95)

These are one of the most important of the futures contracts. You need to learn about eurodollar futures.

Section 6.3 Stock Index Futures (page 98)

You need to understand how the S&P 500 future works.

The summary section beginning on page 99 is quite detailed. If you feel comfortable with this reading you need not go through this.

Question practice

- Attempt practice problems 1 to 5 and 7 to 9 starting on page 101.
- In addition, all questions in the BPP Question Bank should be attempted prior to the exam.

2 hours

STUDY SESSION 17 – READING 60

Option Markets and Contracts (page 107)

3 hours

Key areas

The key thing is to understand the concept of options, the different sorts and the basic pay offs. You are as likely to be asked a factual or descriptive question as a numerical one. It is less daunting than you might believe if you have never studied options before.

- Characteristics

- 'Moneyness'

- Payoffs

- Factors affecting options

Content review – CFA curriculum

Section 2 Basic Definitions (page 108-112)

Read and understand the option terminology in section 2.1 (page 109) , this is very important as is understanding the concept of 'moneyness' in section 2.3 (page 111).

Section 3 Structure of Global Option Markets (pages 112-116)

This section can be read through very quickly.

Section 4 Types of Options (pages 116-122)

This section can also be read through quickly, there is little that can be examined.

Section 5 Principles of Option Pricing (pages 123-143)

This is a more complex section, if you really struggle with the terminology then focus on the definitions and the payoff graphs in exhibit 5 (page 125). Attempt the questions in example 1 (page 126) after reading this section, if you can do these you have the key part of the section covered.

2 hours

Boundary conditions in section 5.2 (page 128) are of less importance. Just focus on the core concepts not the detail.

Sections 5.3 (pages 133) and 5.4 (pages 134) should be understood, especially the concept of time value.

Section 5.5 (page 135) on put-call parity is an area that a lot of students struggle with. The key things are to understand the terminology of what is meant by, fiduciary calls, protective puts, put-call parity and synthetic options. If you are struggling with the calculations then it is not worth spending lots of time on these, just focus on the definitions.

The remainder of the chapter can be read through quickly, it is worth trying to remember the Greek names in section 5.9 (page 143) as this could be an easy mark.

The summary on page 143 is very detailed and can be missed out.

Question practice

- Attempt practice problems 1 to 5 and 8 to 19 starting on page 147.

1 hour

- In addition, all questions in the BPP Question Bank should be attempted prior to the exam.

STUDY SESSION 17 – READING 61

Swap Markets and Contracts (page 155)

3 hours

Key areas

This is a short section which is relatively easy reading. There is little in the way of calculations to be made, it is largely about understanding the basic mechanics and cash flows of swaps.

- Basic characteristics of swaps
- Cash flows of a swap

Content review – CFA curriculum

Section 1 Characteristics and Termination (pages 155-158)

Read through these sections making sure you understand what is meant by the definitions in bold. Know the four ways to terminate a swap.

Section 2 Global Markets (pages 158-159)

This section can be ignored.

2 hours

Section 3 Types of Swaps (pages 159-171)

Read through this section carefully making sure you understand what is meant by the different sorts of swaps and how the cash flow streams work. Make sure in particular you understand how the floating or variable cash flows are calculated and which reference rate is used to calculate each cash flow. This sometimes catches students out.

The summary on page 172 can be ignored.

Question practice

- Attempt practice problems 2 and 7 to 12, at the back of this reading from page 173.

1 hour

STUDY SESSION 17 – READING 62

Risk Management Applications of Option Strategies (page 179) **3 hours**

Importance level **High**

Key areas

- This section is a follow on from Reading 63 and combines a number of concepts
- Payoff graphs
- Valuations

Content review – CFA curriculum

Section 2 Option Strategies for Equity Portfolios (pages 180-196)

There is only one section which covers everything. You should work your way through the reading in particular using the graphs to cement your understanding. Some of the narrative on covered calls and protective puts can be glossed over. **2 hours**

The summary is a short revision guide and can be found on pages 196-7.

Question practice

- Attempt all 8 practice problems at the back of this reading on page 199. They cover the potential range of examinable topics in this area. **1 hour**

- In addition, all questions in the BPP Question Bank should be attempted prior to the exam.

CHECKPOINT – END OF STUDY SESSION 17

You are now able to attempt **Progress Test 9 on Derivatives**.

2 hours

BPP
LEARNING MEDIA

Progress Test 9 – Derivatives

Questions

1. The minimum tick size for a eurodollar futures contract is:
    A. $12.50.
    B. $25.00.
    C. $50.00.

2. An investor buys a stock at $40, buys a put option on the stock at a strike price of $39 (with a premium of $2) and writes a call option on the stock at a strike of $42 (with a premium of $1). The investor's gain or loss if the stock price moves to $46 is *closest to*:
    A. $6 profit.
    B. $1 profit.
    C. $5 loss.

3. Which of the following is *most appropriate* for stock call options?
    A. An American option is always worth more than a European option.
    B. A European option is always worth more than an American option.
    C. An American option may be worth more than a European option.

4. An investor concerned about a fall in equity markets would:
    A. Buy a portfolio of aggressive stocks.
    B. Sell stock index futures to protect his underlying equity position.
    C. Leverage up his equity investment by borrowing money.

5. Which of the following trades would be the *most appropriate* for an investor who is intending to deposit money in three months' time?
    A. Buy an interest rate call option.
    B. Sell a FRA.
    C. Sell an interest rate future.

6. A fund manager has been given the opportunity to undertake tactical asset allocation by the plan sponsor of a pension plan. He believes that equity markets are most likely to fall heavily in the near future but there is a significant probability of high volatility in either direction. Which of the following strategies is *most appropriate* to hedge his position?
    A. Covered call.
    B. Protective put.
    C. Long index future.

7. An investor has just written a covered call at a strike of 15 and a premium of 1. The share price is currently 10. At what share price does the investor break even?

    A. 9.

    B. 11.

    C. 14.

8. A 2 × 6 FRA is quoted at 3%. An investor buys the FRA based on a notional principal of $1m. The following interest rates occur.

	120-day LIBOR	150-day LIBOR	180-day LIBOR
In 30 days' Time	3.2%	3.3%	3.4%
In 60 days' Time	3.25%	3.35%	3.45%
In 90 days' Time	3.3%	3.4%	3.5%

    If an investor buys this FRA, the amount she will receive from the seller of the FRA at expiry is *closest to*:

    A. $824.

    B. $833.

    C. $2,212.

9. Which of the following strategies is *most likely* to be a suitable hedge for an airline company exposed to the cost of oil?

    A. A short forward contract on oil will ensure that if the price of oil falls, the value of the company will rise.

    B. A long put on oil forward contracts will enable the company to sell oil and profit when the oil price falls.

    C. A long call on oil forward contracts will enable the company to benefit from oil price falls and give a price ceiling when oil prices rise.

10. Which of the following call options is mispriced?

Exercise Price	Expiration		
	Jan	April	July
70	20	24	27
80	12	20	19
90	3	4	5
100	1	2	3

    The stock price is 85.

    A. April 80.

    B. Jan 90.

    C. April 70.

11. Which of the following *best describes* a protective put?

    A. An investor is long stock and buys a call option on the stock to create a put profile.

    B. An investor is long stock and sells a call option on the stock to create a put profile.

    C. An investor is long stock and buys a put option on the stock.

12. A put on Stock X with a strike price of $40 is priced at $2.00 per share; while a call with a strike price of $40 is priced at $3.50. What is the maximum per share loss to the writer of the uncovered put and the maximum per share gain to the writer of the uncovered call?

	MAXIMUM LOSS TO PUT WRITER	MAXIMUM GAIN TO CALL WRITER
A.	$38.00	$3.50
B.	$38.00	$36.50
C.	$40.00	$3.50

13. If stock prices in general are expected to increase substantially after the transaction is completed, which of the following transactions in the stock index option market would be *most risky* for an investor to undertake?

    A. Buying a call option.

    B. Writing an uncovered put option.

    C. Writing an uncovered call option.

14. Which of the following statements is *least accurate*?

    A. An American option cannot be worth less than a European option.

    B. The value of a call cannot be worth less than the value of the underlying stock.

    C. The value of a long dated call cannot be less than the value of a short dated call.

15. A fund manager arranges an equity swap with a dealer based on a notional principal of $10m with payments made semiannually. The fund manager pays the dealer the return on a mid-cap stock index which is currently 1,261 and in six months' time moves to 1,027. The dealer pays a fixed rate of 7%. Assuming that a 30/360 day count is used, what are the cash flows due at the end of the first six months?

    A. The dealer pays the fund manager $2,205,670.

    B. The fund manager pays the dealer $1,505,670.

    C. The fund manager pays the dealer $577,835.

16. Which of the following is a criticism of the derivatives markets?

    A. They allow arbitrageurs to exploit price differences to make profits.

    B. They introduce risk into the underlying spot market due to the profit-seeking actions of hedges.

    C. They create complex products that end users may not adequately understand.

17. Which one of the following statements is *most appropriate* for swaps?

A. They are exchange-traded instruments.

B. They are marked to market daily.

C. There is credit risk.

18. An investor buys a stock at a price of $40.00. At the same time, he writes a European call option on the above stock. The call option has a strike price of $42.00 and a premium of $2.50. If the stock price is $43.20 when the call option expires, the overall gain to the investor is:

A. $2.00.

B. $2.50.

C. $4.50.

19. Upon opening a futures position, an initial margin of $5,000 was deposited. The maintenance margin level is set at $2,700. Which of the following losses over the first day would result in a margin call of $2,400?

A. $100.

B. $2,400.

C. $2,600.

20. Which one of the following contracts is *most likely* to require a conversion factor?

A. Currency forward.

B. American call option.

C. Treasury bond future.

21. Which of the following would *least likely* be a reason for an index futures contract failing to give a perfect hedge for a portfolio of stocks?

A. Incorrectly assessing the beta of the portfolio.

B. Unsystematic risk in the portfolio.

C. Unsystematic risk in the futures contract.

22. Which of the following statements is *most accurate*?

A. An investor holding a stock portfolio can protect their capital value by writing call options on stocks.

B. A short call stock option position reacts favorably to time decay.

C. A short call can be constructed by having a long future and a long put.

23. Which of the following is the maximum value of a call stock option with two months to expiry?

A. The strike price.

B. The stock price.

C. The stock price less the strike price.

24. Which one of the following transactions is *most appropriate* for an investor wishing to lock in a deposit rate?

    A. Buy FRA.

    B. Sell FRA.

    C. Buy floor.

25. An investor has entered into a semiannual interest rate swap, paying 8% fixed and receiving LIBOR. LIBOR is now 9%. The notional principal of the swap is $1m. What is the cash flow to the investor under the swap?

    A. Receive $5,000.

    B. Receive $10,000.

    C. Pay $5,000.

26. The credit risk of a futures contract is most like that of a:

    A. Stock.

    B. Exchange-traded option.

    C. Corporate bond.

27. Which of the following is a type of contingent claim?

    A. Option.

    B. Forward contract.

    C. Future.

28. Which one of the following *most accurately* explains how standardization of futures contracts promote liquidity?

    A. There is no clearing house.

    B. Contract expirations are universal.

    C. Contract quantities are determined by counterparties.

29. A call option is out-of-the-money when the:

    A. Value of the underlying asset exceeds the exercise price.

    B. Value of the underlying asset is less than the exercise price.

    C. Option has been sold, and a profit has been claimed.

30. Which of the following would not be used as a means of settling obligations under a forward contract?

    A. Cash settlement.

    B. Physical delivery.

    C. Exchange for physical.

BPP
LEARNING MEDIA

Progress Test 9 – Derivatives

Answers

1. **B**   This represents a change in the underlying three month interest rate (annualised) of 1 basis point

     Do not confuse this with the STIR future, the U.K. equivalent, which has a tick of £12.50

     See LOS 59f

2. **B**

Stock	+6
Put	−2
Call	−3
	+1

     See LOS 62a

3. **C**   If the right to early exercise is not advantageous, an American may only be worth the same as a European option, not worth more

     See LOS 60k

4. **B**   Sell futures or buy put options to hedge a long cash market position

     See LOS 59f

5. **B**   As the investor is depositing money, he will be concerned that interest rates are going to fall. Therefore, he needs a derivative that will make money if interest rates fall. Remember that interest rate futures are quoted as 100 − LIBOR, so if interest rates fall they will increase in value. This means that they move in the same direction as bond futures

     See LOS 58f, 59f and 60f

6. **B**   Long the underlying and long put. This gives downside protection while still offering upside participation

     See LOS 62b

7. **A**   The investor has received a premium of $1. If the share price falls to $9, he loses $1 on the share, meaning that he breaks even overall

     See LOS 62b

8. **A**   A 2 × 6 FRA expires in two months' time and the period that its interest rate refers to is the four months after expiry. The relevant rate is therefore 3.25%

     $$\$1,000,000 \times (3.25\% - 3\%) \times \frac{120}{360} = \$833$$

     $$\frac{\$833}{1+\left(3.25\% \times \frac{120}{360}\right)} = \$824$$

     See LOS 58g

9. **C** The company is more concerned with a rise in the oil price. It should therefore hedge its exposure by buying oil forward/futures contracts, or buying a long call on oil/oil forward contracts

   See LOS 59a and b

10. **A** This is overpriced relative to the July 80. The July 80 should have greater time value

    See LOS 60i

11. **C** They long put allows the investor to sell the stock at the strike price and protects the investor against falls in the stock price

    See LOS 62b

12. **A** The put buyer could theoretically earn $40 – 0 – $2 = $38, so $38 is also the put seller's maximum loss. The call writer would earn only the option premium of $3.50

    See LOS 62a

13. **C** Most risky = Greatest loss

    An uncovered call option written before stock prices increase substantially would mean that the option would be exercised by the buyer. The loss would be the cost of acquiring the stock less exercise price, offset by the premium received

    See LOS 62a

14. **B** The value of a call cannot be greater than the value of the stock

    See LOS 60k

15. **A** The fixed payment from the dealer to the fund manager is $10m $\times$ 7% $\times \dfrac{180}{360}$ = $350,000

    The equity payment is $\left(\dfrac{1,027}{1,261} - 1 \right) \times \$10m = -\$1,855,670$

    Since the fund manager pays the equity return and it is negative, the dealer must pay the equity return. So the dealer pays

    $1,855,670 + $350,000 = $2,205,670

    See LOS 61b

16. **C** The presence of arbitrageurs is seen as a boost to market efficiency. Although there is concern that derivatives may cause, on occasion, movements in the spot market, it is not due to hedgers seeking profits as hedgers are trying to minimise risk

    See LOS 57c

17. **C** Swaps are OTC instruments and as such are less heavily regulated than traded future contracts

    See LOS 57a

18. **C** This is a covered call position where the call sold is out-of-the-money. Since the stock price is greater than the strike price at the option expiry date, the holder of the call will exercise it. Investor is the writer of the call and will have to deliver the stock in exchange for the strike price of $42

Gain on stock = 41 − 40 = 2

Option on premium = 2.50

Total gain to investor = 4.50

See LOS 62a

19. **B** Margin would be called to replenish the account back up to $5,000

See LOS 59c

20. **C** Because the actual bond delivered is one of a selection, so the price of the future is adjusted accordingly

See LOS 59f

21. **C** There is no unsystematic risk in the futures contract as it is linked to a broad stock index

See LOS 59f

22. **B** Decay helps writers and hurts holders of options. A is a covered call position. In C, a long future and a long put can be combined to give the payoff of a long call

See LOS 62b, 60l and 60m

23. **B** No one would pay more for the call than the value of the stock itself

See LOS 60a, 60l ad 60m

24. **B** Futures allow investors to lock in or hedge positions. Selling an FRA would enable a depositor to lock in (a particular LIBOR rate)

See LOS 58f

25. **A** Receiving LIBOR, therefore receive 1% × $1m × ½ = $5,000

See LOS 61b

26. **B** The credit risk of a futures contract is most like that of an option because they are both bought and sold through clearing houses. This forces all of the credit risk to be held by the clearing house

See LOS 59a and 59b

27. **A** The others are types of forward commitments

See LOS 57b

28. **B** Liquidity is promoted in futures contracts by both standardizing quantity and quality. By standardizing quantity there are no 'odd-lot' amounts, and by standardizing quality there are certain standards that all products must comply with. By having these standards investors know what they are getting, and this allows for a market where both buyers and seller are confident and informed about the system

See LOS 59a and 59b

29.   **B**   A call option is considered out-of-the-money if the value of the underlying asset is less than the exercise price. If the value of the underlying stock is greater then the exercise price it is considered in-the-money, and if the value of the underlying stock and the exercise price are equal the value of the option is said to be at-the-money

        See LOS 60c

30.   **C**   Exchange for physicals relates to futures, not forwards

        See LOS 58b

STUDY GUIDANCE

Alternative Investments

This guidance aims to identify the topics that we consider to be of premium importance for your exam preparation.

Study session 18 (Volume 6) comprises of:

Reading 63   Introduction to Alternative Investments

Recommended study time is 4 hours of work. An additional 2 hours should be added to complete Progress Test 10 on Alternative Investments.

 Exam focus

This section represents about 5% of the exam. Given the small percentage of this section, you should plan your revision accordingly and not allocate more than the necessary time to this area, focusing on the key points only.

 Pre-requisites

Basic quantitative applications (Study Session 2) should have been studied.

Key areas

This section covers all of the Alternative Investment area. This section will cover 5% of the exam. Given time constraints it is important to focus on the key points only within each area. Note also that this reading has been updated for the 2014 sitting (commodities had spent some years in a separate reading but is now back in with the rest of alternatives in Reading 63).

- Alternative investments versus traditional investments
- Hedge funds
- Private equity
- Real estate
- Contango and backwardation
- Commodity controversies
- Commodity strategies

Content review – CFA curriculum

Section 2 Alternative Investments (page 210)

This section introduces alternative investments, describing their characteristics, how they can be used in a diversified portfolio, and how to actually invest to gain exposure to alternative investments. Focus on being able to list and describe the categories of alternative investment in section 2.1 (page 214) and in section 2.3 (page 217) their diversifying potential is explored.

Section 3 Hedge Funds (page 219)

As you go through each type of alternative investment focus on the learning outcome statement which requires you to look at strategies; sub-categories; benefits and risks; fee structure; due diligence; return measurement and valuation.

It is important to recognize and be able to identify the various hedge fund strategies from section 3.1 (page 222) as this can be an easy mark in the exam.

Specifically for hedge funds you also need to fully understand management, incentive fees, and net-of-fees returns. This is covered in section 3.3.1 (page 226) and gets tested comprehensively in example 2 on page 227.   **3 hours**

Section 4 Private Equity (Venture Capital) (page 235)

Understand the stages of venture capital investing and the definitions of the different stages. You must also understand the investment strategies used in private equity and, in particular, the potential risks as covered in section 4.3 on page 241.

Portfolio company valuation in section 4.4 on page 243 is a revisit of DCF and multiple approaches that you have seen already in Reading 41.

Section 5 Real Estate

This section needs a quick read through and again in section 5.4 (page 251) on valuation, you should recognize the valuation concepts. There is no need to perform any calculations here.

Section 6 Commodities

This section should be read through completely, particular focus should be paid to the approximation of future costs formula on page 259.

Sections 7 and 8 (pages 260-265)

Only a quick read through is needed here. The most important point to grasp in section 8 is that traditional risk/return measures may not be adequate to assess alternative investments. Therefore, distinct risk management processes need to be in place for different types of alternative investments incorporating due diligence procedures in section 8.3 on page 263 or covered rather comprehensively in exhibit 20 on page 264.

The summary on page 265 is detailed and need not be read.

Question practice

- As this is an updated reading for the 2014 sitting, attempt all 14 practice problems.

- In addition, all questions in the BPP Question Bank should be attempted prior to the exam.

1 hour

CHECKPOINT – END OF STUDY SESSION 18

You are now able to attempt **Progress Test 10 on Alternative Investments**. **2 hours**

Progress Test 10 – Alternative Investments

Questions

1. Which of the following is least likely to be associated with alternative investments?

    A. Long-only investments.

    B. Use of leverage.

    C. Active investment strategy.

2. Which of the following is *least accurate* of direct investment in real estate?

    A. It is a liquid asset.

    B. It is relatively difficult to value.

    C. Leveraging of returns is possible.

3. Which of the following *best* describes the real estate valuation method that estimates annual net operating income and discounts to present value using a capitalisation rate?

    A. Comparable sales approach.

    B. Income approach.

    C. Cost approach.

4. Which of the following is *least* likely to be a reason for an investor to add alternative investments to their portfolio?

    A. Increased diversification.

    B. Increase in risk/return profile.

    C. Increased investor confidence from market regulation.

5. An investor wishes to use both long and short strategies, use high leverage, and generate positive returns even when the broad market performance is generating negative returns. Which of the following would be the *most* suitable alternative investment for the investor?

    A. Hedge fund.

    B. Real estate.

    C. Commodities.

6. Which one of the following characteristics is *least appropriate* for describing an investment in commodity derivatives?

    A. Potential for inflation protection.

    B. Provides diversification benefits.

    C. Weakly correlated to the supply-demand dynamics of an underlying commodity.

7. Which of the following statements about investment in timberland is *least accurate*?

    A. Timber can easily be grown but storage can be costly.

    B. Income stream from timberland has historically not been highly correlated with other asset classes.

    C. The three primary return drivers for timberland are biological growth, commodity price changes, and land price changes.

8. Which of the following investment strategy is *most* likely to offer potential high alpha returns for an investor?

    A. Long-only passive investment in traditional assets.

    B. Concentrated portfolio strategy.

    C. Active style bias strategy.

9. A hedge fund strategy that seeks to profit from changes in corporate restructuring and acquisitions is *best* known as:

    A. An event-driven strategy.

    B. A relative-value strategy.

    C. An equity hedge strategy.

10. Which of the following is *closest* to the definition of funds from operations (FFO) used in the income-based approach to REIT valuations?

    A. Net income plus depreciation.

    B. Net income plus depreciation less recurring capex.

    C. Net income plus depreciation less gains from property sales plus losses from property sales.

11. Which of the following best describes why a 'side pocket' is used in a hedge fund?

    A Gives the hedge fund the ability to invest a small percentage of funds outside of a stated strategy.

    B. Gives the hedge fund the ability to invest in other hedge funds.

    C. Gives the hedge fund the ability to charge non-incentive fees on part of its assets.

12. Which of the following best describes the following hedge fund strategy? 'Take long positions in identified undervalued securities, take short positions in identified overvalued securities, whilst maintaining beta of approximately zero.'

    A. Fundamental value.

    B. Fundamental growth.

    C. Market neutral.

13. Which of the following is the *least likely* to be a factor that can magnify losses for hedge funds?

    A. Redemptions.

    B. Leverage.

    C. Use of a high water mark

14. Which of the following finance techniques would be *most appropriate* to finance a new idea that is not yet at the marketing or production stage?

    A. Seed finance.

    B. Early stage finance.

    C. LBO finance.

15. A hedge fund that takes bets on the direction of the exchange rate movement is *most* likely:

    A. A long short fund.

    B. A global macro fund.

    C. An event driven fund.

16. PEI, a private equity firm, is looking to invest in a mail order company, NextDay Inc that has an EBITDA of $72 million. A search of recent transactions shows that three mail order companies have been sold in the last year for 6x EBITDA, 4x EBITDA and 8xEBITDA. Based on this information, which of the following is most likely to be the highest valuation that the PEI will place on Nextday Inc?

    A. $432m.

    B. $576m.

    C. $504m.

17. In calculating hedge fund fees, which one of the following statements *best* describes the use of a soft hurdle rate?

    A. An incentive fee is based on the returns in excess of a hurdle rate.

    B. An incentive fee is based on the entire fund return.

    C. There are no incentive fees.

18. Which of the following is least likely to be a characteristic of an equity hedge strategy for a hedge fund?

    A. Significant use of leverage is common.

    B. Fund aims for market neutrality.

    C. Fund makes bets on valuation differences.

19. When the futures price is higher than the spot price, the market is said to be in what state?

    A. Normal.

    B. Contango.

    C. Backwardation.

20. Which of the following is the *least likely* method of valuing real estate?

   A. Comparative sales.

   B. Income approach.

   C. Appraisal approach.

21. Which of the following is *least* likely to be a benefit of an investment in a fund of hedge funds compared to a hedge fund?

   A. Cheaper fees.

   B. Access to closed funds.

   C. Due diligence on individual funds.

22. Which of the following is *least accurate* of a REIT?

   A. Its shares are quoted on a stock exchange.

   B. It is means of directly investing in property.

   C. It may invest in either real estate or mortgages.

23. The impact on a portfolio of traditional asset of introducing direct commodity investments is *most likely* to be:

   A. A reduction in long term volatility as a result of the high positive correlation between commodities and traditional asset classes.

   B. An increase in long term return as a result of the positive roll return earned when the market is in contango.

   C. A reduction in exposure to inflation risk, particularly for institutional investors such as pension funds and foundations.

24. A hedge fund which invests in securities of companies in bankruptcy would *best* be described as a fund following which kind of strategy?

   A. Event-driven.

   B. Relative value.

   C. Equity hedge.

25. Which of the following is *least likely* to be accurate when comparing investing in hedge funds with investing in private equity funds?

   A. Both are structured as partnerships.

   B. Both have management fees calculated as a percentage of assets under management .

   C. Both provide diversification benefits to a traditional asset portfolio.

26. Which of the following is *not* a similarity between distressed investing and venture capital funds?

   A. Direct investors should have some management knowledge.

   B. They are usually illiquid.

   C. Investment is often in new businesses.

27. Which of the following is *most likely* to be an advantage of investing in a fund of funds (FOF)?

    A. Reduced risk due to diversification.

    B. Higher returns than investing in hedge funds directly.

    C. Easy to chose funds due to transparency of performance reporting.

28. A hedge fund currently has a value of $10m. The fees are a management fee of 3% of the value of the fund at the beginning of the year plus an incentive fee of 20% on any returns in excess of a watermark value of $11m. If the fund earns a return of 28% in the next year, how much will the total management fees be?

    A. $860,000.

    B. $616,000.

    C. $660,000.

29. Which of the following investments is most likely to offer the *smallest* exposure to commodities?

    A. Investment swap contract based on future commodity prices.

    B. An equity share in an ETF (exchange traded fund) that invests in commodities.

    C. A share in an oil company.

30. Which of the following risk measures is likely to be the *most* appropriate when considering the downside risk of investing in alternative investments?

    A. Value at Risk combined with stress testing.

    B. Sortino ratio.

    C. Sharpe ratio.

Progress Test 10 – Alternative Investments

Answers

1. **A** Long-only investments are associated with traditional investments such as stocks and bonds

   See LOS 63a

2. **A** Real estate is particularly illiquid compared to traditional asset classes

   See LOS 63d

3. **B** Dividing NOI by a capitalisation rate is called the direct capitalisation approach and is an example of an income approach to real estate valuation

   See LOS 63e

4. **C** Alternative investment markets tend to have low regulation and less transparency

   See LOS 63a

5. **A** Long and short strategies, use of high leverage, and generating positive returns even when the broad market performance is down, is characteristic of hedge funds

   See LOS 63b

6. **C** Commodity derivative prices are a function of the underlying commodity prices and are highly correlated. It is therefore important to understand the supply-demand dynamics of the underlying commodity as this will directly impact the commodity derivative price

   See LOS 63d

7. **A** Timber can be easily stored by not harvesting. This feature is a benefit and not a cost

   See LOS 63d

8. **B** Concentrated portfolio strategies have few securities which could outperform the market and achieve higher returns. They are renowned for being attractive to investors because of their high-alpha potential. Passive strategies aim to generate beta returns rather than alpha returns. Active style biases are highly correlated with the market and tend to generate beta returns rather than alpha returns

   See LOS 63d

9. **A** Relative-value strategy seeks to profit from pricing discrepancy. Equity hedge strategies take long and short positions in equity and equity derivatives

   See LOS 63d

10. **C** FFO starts with net income and adds back depreciation because it is a non cash item. Additionally, it adjusts for profits/losses on property sales as they are considered non-recurring

    See LOS 63d

11. A   A side pocket allows a hedge fund to invest 20% or less of its assets into when and what it sees fit, not constrained by its stated strategy

See LOS 63d

12. C   Fundamental value takes long positions only in undervalued securities. Fundamental growth invests in securities with high growth and likely capital appreciation

See LOS 63d

13. C   Redemptions can magnify losses because the manager may have to liquidate assets to facilitate the redemption and this can incur transaction costs. Leverage always magnifies losses/gains. A high water mark is used to calculate fee income and is not linked to magnifying losses

See LOS 63d

14. A   This is for the start-up of a new venture

See LOS 63d

15. B   Event driven funds invest in companies or securities based on events such as bankruptcy. Long short funds hold long and short positions in securities

See LOS 63d

16. B   The highest multiple is used, not an average. Giving $8 \times \$72m = \$576m$

See LOS 63e

17. B   A hard hurdle rate is described in option A. A soft hurdle rate describes incentive fees charged on the whole return, ie effectively no hurdle

See LOS 63d

18. B   An equity hedge strategy is not necessarily market neutral. They may have a systematic short selling bias or vary their positions based on market views

See LOS 63d

19. B   A contango market is where the futures price is higher than the spot price

See LOS 63d

20. C

See LOS 63e

21. A   The fees are higher because in addition to the individual hedge fund fees, the investor has to pay the fees of the fund of funds

See LOS 63d

22. B   It is indirect investment

See LOS 63d

23. **C** Commodities can reduce portfolio volatility, but this is due to low correlation, not high. A positive roll return is experienced when markets are in backwardation

See LOS 63b

24. **A**

See LOS 63d

25. **B** Management fees are calculated differently. Management fees for private equity investment is a percentage of committed capital. Only when the committed capital is invested is the management fee based on invested capital/funds under management

See LOS 63d

26. **C** Distressed securities may be long-standing businesses that are close to filing for bankruptcy

See LOS 63d

27. **A** A fund of funds will invest in a variety of hedge funds, allowing an investor to diversify. However, the fund manager will charge a fee for this and due to the diversification process, returns are often lower than investing directly in hedge funds

See LOS 63d

28. **C** Management fee = 3% × $10m = $300,000

Fund value at year-end = $10m × 1.28 = $12.8m

Incentive fee = ($12.8m – $11m) × 20% = $360,000

Total management fees = $300,000 + $360,000 = $660,000

See LOS 63f

29. **C** Common stocks of oil companies do not solely track the underlying performance of oil but are impacted by many other factors and are therefore only likely to give investors a small exposure to derivatives

See LOS 63d

30. **A** The Sharpe ratio is not a downside risk measurement. The Sortino ratio uses deviation in its calculation and for the non-normal returns of alternative investments, may give a skewed result. VAR uses standard deviation so results can also be skewed but when combined with stress testing under different scenarios, will give the clearest picture of downside risk

See LOS 63g